Data Analysis with Python. An Introduction

Data Analysis with Python: An Introduction
(c) 2023 Holger Speckter

Disclaimer

The information in this book has been compiled with great care and attention to accuracy. However, the author and publisher make no warranties or representations regarding its completeness or accuracy. Use the information at your own risk; the author and publisher shall not be liable for any damages, including without limitation, indirect or consequential damages, arising from the use of this book. It is your responsibility to verify any information before relying on it. This book is for educational purposes only and not a substitute for professional advice.

Table of Contents

Index
- Chapter 1: Introduction to Python
- Chapter 2: Getting Started with Python
- Chapter 3: Essential Python Programming
- Chapter 4: Data Handling with Python
- Chapter 5: Advanced Data Manipulation
- Chapter 6: Data Visualisation
- Chapter 7: Statistical Analysis with Python
- Chapter 8: Introduction to Machine Learning
- Chapter 9: Working with Text Data
- Chapter 10: Time Series Analysis
- Chapter 11: Advanced Topics
- Chapter 12: Practical Projects and Applications
- Chapter 13: Best Practices and Further Resources

Chapter 1: Introduction to Python

Why Python is the Ideal Choice

Python is a versatile, high-level programming language known for its simplicity, readability, and vast ecosystem. Over the years, Python has become the language of choice for many developers, data scientists, and organisations due to its wide range of applications, including web development, data analysis, artificial intelligence, scientific computing, and more.

Key reasons why Python stands out:

Easy to Learn and Use: Python's syntax is clear and readable, making it an excellent choice for beginners. Its design philosophy emphasises code readability and simplicity, which allows new programmers to pick up the language quickly. Experienced developers also appreciate Python for its ability to write complex programs efficiently with fewer lines of code compared to other languages.

Versatile and Flexible: Python supports multiple programming paradigms, including procedural, object-oriented, and functional programming. This flexibility allows developers to choose the best approach for their projects, making Python suitable for a wide range of tasks, from scripting small automation scripts to developing large-scale enterprise applications.

Extensive Libraries and Frameworks: One of Python's greatest strengths is its rich ecosystem of libraries and frameworks. For data analysis and manipulation, libraries like Pandas, NumPy, and SciPy are widely used. For web development, frameworks like Django and Flask provide powerful tools to build robust web applications. For machine learning and artificial intelligence, TensorFlow, Keras, and PyTorch offer comprehensive solutions for building and deploying models.

Strong Community Support: Python has a large and active community that contributes to its vast collection of resources, tutorials, and third-party modules. This community support makes it easier to find help, share knowledge, and collaborate on projects. Python's extensive documentation and numerous online forums, such as Stack Overflow, further assist developers in solving problems and improving their skills.

Cross-Platform Compatibility: Python is a cross-platform language that runs on various operating systems, including Windows, macOS, and Linux. This compatibility ensures that Python code can be written and executed on different platforms without modification, making it highly portable and versatile.

Integration Capabilities: Python integrates well with other languages and technologies. It can be easily combined with C, C++, Java, and other languages, allowing developers to leverage existing codebases and optimize performance-critical components. Python's ability to interface with various databases, web services, and APIs makes it an ideal choice for building complex, integrated systems.

Python: A Brief History

Python was created in the late 1980s by Guido van Rossum, a Dutch programmer who was inspired by the British comedy series "Monty Python's Flying Circus." Guido aimed to develop a language that emphasized code readability and simplicity, enabling programmers to write clear and logical code for both small and large-scale projects.

Key milestones in Python's history:

Python 1.0 (1991): The first official release of Python introduced basic data types and constructs, such as strings, lists, and dictionaries, along with support for functions, modules, and exceptions. This version laid the foundation for Python's development and established its core philosophy.

Python 2.0 (2000): This release added significant features, including list comprehensions, garbage collection, and support for Unicode. Python 2.x became widely adopted and remained the standard for many years. The release of Python 2.7 in 2010 marked the final version of the 2.x series, which continued to receive support until 2020.

Python 3.0 (2008): Python 3.0 was a major revision of the language, designed to address inconsistencies and improve the language's design. It introduced changes that were not backward-compatible with Python 2.x, requiring developers to update their code. Key enhancements included print function changes, integer division modifications, and improvements to string handling and standard library modules.

Python 3.x Series: Since the release of Python 3.0, the language has continued to evolve with regular updates. Each new version brings enhancements, performance improvements, and additional features. The Python Software Foundation, the organisation responsible for maintaining Python, ensures that the language remains modern and capable of meeting the needs of the developer community.

Python's journey from its inception to its current status as one of the most popular programming languages is a testament to its design and the strength of its community. Python has consistently adapted to the changing landscape of software development, maintaining its relevance and appeal across various industries.

Overview of Python's Features and Applications

Python's features make it an ideal choice for a wide range of applications, from simple scripting to complex data analysis and web development. Let's explore some of the core features that contribute to Python's versatility:

1. Interpreted Language: Python is an interpreted language, which means that Python code is executed line by line by the Python interpreter. This allows for quick testing and debugging, making development faster and more efficient. Unlike compiled languages, Python does not require a separate compilation step, streamlining the development process.

2. Dynamic Typing: In Python, variables do not require explicit declaration of their data types. The type of a variable is determined at runtime, allowing for more flexibility in coding. This dynamic typing system simplifies the development process and reduces the amount of boilerplate code needed.

3. Extensive Standard Library: Python's standard library includes modules for handling a wide range of tasks, such as file I/O, system calls, internet protocols, and data serialisation. This extensive library allows developers to accomplish many tasks without relying on external libraries, making Python a powerful tool out of the box.

4. Cross-Platform Compatibility: Python runs on various operating systems, including Windows, macOS, and

Linux. This cross-platform compatibility ensures that Python code can be developed and executed on different systems without modification. Python's portability makes it an attractive choice for projects that need to run on multiple platforms.

5. Readable and Maintainable Code: Python's syntax is designed to be clean and readable, promoting best practices in code writing. The use of indentation to define code blocks enforces consistent formatting, which improves code readability and maintainability. Python's emphasis on readability makes it easier for teams to collaborate and review each other's code.

6. Support for Multiple Programming Paradigms: Python supports various programming paradigms, including procedural, object-oriented, and functional programming. This flexibility allows developers to choose the most suitable approach for their projects. Object-oriented programming (OOP) in Python enables the creation of reusable and modular code, while functional programming allows for concise and expressive code.

7. Strong Community and Ecosystem: Python's large and active community contributes to its extensive ecosystem of libraries, frameworks, and tools. The Python Package Index (PyPI) hosts thousands of third-party packages that extend Python's functionality, covering areas such as web development, data analysis, machine learning, and more. This vibrant community ensures that Python

remains up-to-date with the latest developments in technology.

Applications of Python:

Python's versatility makes it suitable for a wide range of applications across different industries. Here are some common use cases:

1. Web Development: Python is widely used for web development, thanks to frameworks like Django and Flask. These frameworks provide tools and libraries to build robust web applications quickly. Django, a high-level framework, includes built-in features for authentication, database management, and URL routing, making it ideal for large-scale applications. Flask, a micro-framework, offers more flexibility and is suitable for smaller projects or applications that require custom components.

2. Data Analysis and Visualisation: Python is a popular choice for data analysis and visualisation due to libraries like Pandas, NumPy, and Matplotlib. Pandas provide data structures and functions for data manipulation and analysis, while NumPy offers support for numerical computations. Matplotlib and Seaborn enable the creation of various types of visualisations, helping data scientists explore and communicate their findings effectively.

3. Machine Learning and Artificial Intelligence: Python's rich ecosystem includes powerful libraries and frameworks for machine learning and AI, such as

TensorFlow, Keras, and PyTorch. These tools allow developers to build, train, and deploy machine learning models with ease. Scikit-Learn, another popular library, offers a range of machine learning algorithms and utilities for data preprocessing, model selection, and evaluation.

4. Scientific Computing: Python is extensively used in scientific computing and research. Libraries like SciPy and SymPy provide tools for scientific and mathematical computations, while Jupyter Notebooks offer an interactive environment for conducting experiments and sharing results. Python's ability to handle complex calculations and data processing tasks makes it a valuable tool for scientists and researchers.

5. Automation and Scripting: Python's simplicity and ease of use make it an excellent choice for automation and scripting tasks. From automating repetitive tasks to writing scripts for system administration, Python's extensive standard library and third-party modules provide the necessary tools to streamline workflows and improve efficiency.

6. Game Development: Python is also used in game development, with libraries like Pygame providing tools for creating 2D games. While Python may not be the first choice for high-performance game development, it is suitable for prototyping and developing simple games or educational software.

7. Internet of Things (IoT): Python's lightweight nature and ease of use make it a suitable choice for IoT

development. Libraries like MicroPython and CircuitPython allow developers to write Python code for microcontrollers and other embedded devices. Python's ability to interface with hardware components and sensors makes it a popular choice for IoT projects.

8. Financial Technology (FinTech): Python is widely used in the financial industry for tasks such as quantitative analysis, risk management, and algorithmic trading. Libraries like Pandas and NumPy provide tools for data analysis and numerical computations, while libraries like QuantLib offer financial instrument pricing and risk analysis capabilities. Python's ease of use and powerful libraries make it an ideal choice for developing financial models and applications.

Conclusion

Python's journey from its inception to its current status as one of the most popular programming languages is a testament to its design, versatility, and the strength of its community. Python's emphasis on readability, simplicity, and flexibility makes it an ideal choice for both beginners and experienced developers. Its extensive libraries, strong community support, and cross-platform compatibility ensure that Python remains a powerful and relevant tool across various industries and applications.

As you embark on your journey to learn Python, you will discover its potential to simplify complex tasks, automate workflows, and build powerful applications. Whether you are interested in web development, data analysis, machine learning, or any other field, Python provides the tools and resources to help you succeed. Welcome to the world of Python programming, where possibilities are endless, and the only limit is your imagination.

Chapter 2: Getting Started with Python

Installation and Setup

Before you start coding in Python, you need to install it on your computer. Python is available for all major operating systems, including Windows, macOS, and Linux. This section will guide you through the installation process and ensure your development environment is set up correctly.

1. Downloading Python:

- **Windows**:

  - Go to the official Python website: Python Downloads.

    - https://www.python.org/downloads/

  - Click on the "Download Python" button. This will download the latest version of Python.

  - Run the downloaded installer. Ensure you check the box that says "Add Python to PATH" before clicking "Install Now."

- **macOS**:

  - Go to the official Python website: Python Downloads.

    - https://www.python.org/downloads/

  - Click on the "Download Python" button. This will download the latest version of Python.

- Open the downloaded `.pkg` file and follow the instructions to install Python.

- **Linux**:

Python is usually pre-installed on most Linux distributions. You can check if Python is installed by opening a terminal and typing `python3 --version`. If it's not installed, you can install it using your distribution's package manager:

- For Debian-based distributions (like Ubuntu): `sudo apt-get install python3`
- For Red Hat-based distributions (like Fedora): `sudo dnf install python3`

2. Verifying the Installation:

Once Python is installed, verify the installation by opening a terminal (or command prompt on Windows) and typing:

```
python3 --version
```

You should see the version number of the installed Python. Additionally, check if `pip` (Python's package installer) is installed by typing:

```
pip3 --version
```

3. Installing an Integrated Development Environment (IDE):

An Integrated Development Environment (IDE) provides a comprehensive environment for writing, testing, and debugging your Python code. Here are some popular Python IDEs:

- **PyCharm**:
  - Download PyCharm from the JetBrains website.
    - https://www.jetbrains.com/pycharm/download/
  - Follow the installation instructions for your operating system.
  - PyCharm offers both a Community edition (free) and a Professional edition (paid). The Community edition is suitable for most beginners.
- **Visual Studio Code (VS Code)**:
  - Download VS Code from the official website.
    - https://code.visualstudio.com/
  - Follow the installation instructions for your operating system.
  - Once installed, you can enhance VS Code with the Python extension available from the Extensions marketplace.
- **Jupyter Notebook**:
  - Jupyter Notebooks are ideal for data analysis and visualisation tasks.
  - Install Jupyter Notebook using `pip`:

```
pip3 install notebook
```

- Launch Jupyter Notebook by typing `jupyter notebook` in your terminal.

Writing and Running Your First Python Program

Now that you have Python installed, let's write and run your first Python program. We'll start with the classic "Hello, World!" example.

1. Writing the Program:

Open your preferred IDE or a text editor. Create a new file and name it `hello.py`. In this file, type the following code:

```
print("Hello, World!")
```

This simple program uses the `print` function to output the text "Hello, World!" to the screen.

2. Running the Program:

- **Using the Terminal**:

- Open a terminal (or command prompt on Windows).

- Navigate to the directory where you saved `hello.py` using the `cd` command.

- Run the program by typing:

```
python3 hello.py
```

- You should see the output: `Hello, World!`

- **Using an IDE:**
- Open the `hello.py` file in your IDE.
- Most IDEs have a run button (often depicted as a green arrow) that you can click to execute the program.
- The output should appear in the IDE's built-in terminal or output window.

Python Syntax and Basic Concepts

Before diving into more complex programs, it's essential to understand Python's basic syntax and concepts.

1. Variables and Data Types:

Variables are used to store data. Python supports various data types, including integers, floats, strings, and booleans.

```
# Integer
age = 25

# Float
height = 5.9

# String
name = "Alice"

# Boolean
is_student = True
```

2. Comments:

Comments are used to explain code and are ignored by the Python interpreter. Single-line comments start with a #, while multi-line comments are enclosed in triple quotes (""").

```
# This is a single-line comment

"""
This is a
multi-line comment
"""
```

3. Basic Operators:
Python supports various operators for arithmetic, comparison, and logical operations.

– **Arithmetic Operators**:

```
addition = 5 + 3           # 8
subtraction = 10 - 4       # 6
multiplication = 2 * 3     # 6
division = 10 / 2          # 5.0
modulo = 7 % 3             # 1
```

– **Comparison Operators**:

```
equal = (5 == 5)              # True
not_equal = (5 != 3)          # True
greater_than = (7 > 4)        # True
```

```
less_than = (3 < 8)      # True
```

- **Logical Operators:**

```
and_operator = (True and False)   # False
or_operator = (True or False)     # True
not_operator = not(True)          # False
```

4. Control Structures:

Control structures allow you to control the flow of your program. The primary control structures in Python are conditionals and loops.

- **Conditional Statements (if, elif, else):**

```
age = 20

if age >= 18:
    print("You are an adult.")
elif age >= 13:
    print("You are a teenager.")
else:
    print("You are a child.")
```

- **Loops (for, while):**

- **For Loop**:

```
for i in range(5):
    print(i)   # Outputs 0, 1, 2, 3, 4
```

- **While Loop**:

```
count = 0
while count < 5:
    print(count)   # Outputs 0, 1, 2, 3, 4
    count += 1
```

5. Functions and Modules:

Functions are reusable blocks of code that perform a specific task. Modules are collections of functions and variables.

- **Defining and Calling Functions**:

```
def greet(name):
    print(f"Hello, {name}!")

greet("Alice")   # Outputs: Hello, Alice!
```

- **Using Modules**:

```
import math
```

```
result = math.sqrt(16)
print(result)  # Outputs: 4.0
```

Exploring Python Libraries and Packages

Python's strength lies in its extensive library ecosystem. Let's explore some essential libraries that you'll frequently use.

1. NumPy:

NumPy is a library for numerical computations, providing support for arrays and matrices, along with mathematical functions.

– **Installing NumPy**:

```
pip3 install numpy
```

– **Using NumPy**:

```
import numpy as np

array = np.array([1, 2, 3, 4, 5])
print(array)  # Outputs: [1 2 3 4 5]
```

2. Pandas:

Pandas is a powerful library for data manipulation and analysis. It provides data structures like DataFrames for handling structured data.

- **Installing Pandas:**

    ```
    pip3 install pandas
    ```

- **Using Pandas:**

    ```
    import pandas as pd

    data = {'Name': ['Alice', 'Bob',
    'Charlie'], 'Age': [25, 30, 35]}
    df = pd.DataFrame(data)
    print(df)
    ```

3. Matplotlib:
Matplotlib is a library for creating static, animated, and interactive visualisations in Python.

- **Installing Matplotlib:**

    ```
    pip3 install matplotlib
    ```

- **Using Matplotlib:**

    ```
    import matplotlib.pyplot as plt

    x = [1, 2, 3, 4, 5]
    y = [2, 4, 6, 8, 10]
    ```

```
plt.plot(x, y)
plt.xlabel('X-axis')
plt.ylabel('Y-axis')
plt.title('Simple Plot')
plt.show()
```

Setting Up a Virtual Environment

A virtual environment is an isolated environment for Python projects, ensuring that dependencies
are managed separately for each project. This prevents conflicts between different projects' dependencies.
1. Creating a Virtual Environment:

– **Using** venv (included in the Python standard library):

```
python3 -m venv myenv
```

– **Activating the Virtual Environment:**
– **Windows:**

```
myenv\Scripts\activate
```

– **macOS and Linux:**

```
source myenv/bin/activate
```

– **Deactivating the Virtual Environment**:

```
deactivate
```

2. **Managing Dependencies**:

– **Installing Packages**:

```
pip install package_name
```

– **Freezing Dependencies**:

```
pip freeze > requirements.txt
```

– **Installing Dependencies from a File**:

```
pip install -r requirements.txt
```

Debugging and Testing Python Code

Debugging and testing are crucial aspects of software development. Python provides several tools and techniques to help you identify and fix bugs and ensure your code works correctly.

1. **Debugging with** `print` **Statements:**

The simplest way to debug code is by adding `print` statements to output the values of variables and track the program's flow.

```
def add(a, b):
    print(f"a: {a}, b: {b}")   # Debugging line
    return a + b

result = add(3, 4)
print(result)   # Outputs: 7
```

2. Using a Debugger:

IDEs like PyCharm and VS Code have built-in debuggers that allow you to set breakpoints, step through code, and inspect variables.

- **Setting Breakpoints**: Click on the left margin next to the line number in your IDE to set a breakpoint.

- **Starting the Debugger**: Use the debugger icon (often depicted as a bug) in your IDE to start the debugging session.

3. Writing Tests:

Writing tests ensures that your code behaves as expected. Python's built-in `unittest` module provides a framework for writing and running tests.

- **Creating a Test Case**:

```python
import unittest

def add(a, b):
    return a + b

class TestMath(unittest.TestCase):
    def test_add(self):
        self.assertEqual(add(3, 4), 7)
        self.assertEqual(add(-1, 1), 0)
        self.assertEqual(add(0, 0), 0)

if __name__ == '__main__':
    unittest.main()
```

- **Running Tests**: Save the test case in a file (e.g., `test_math.py`) and run it using:

```
python3 test_math.py
```

4. **Using** `pytest`:
`pytest` is a third-party testing framework that simplifies writing and running tests.

- **Installing** `pytest`:

```
pip3 install pytest
```

- **Writing Tests**:

```
def add(a, b):
    return a + b

def test_add():
    assert add(3, 4) == 7
    assert add(-1, 1) == 0
    assert add(0, 0) == 0
```

- **Running Tests**:

```
pytest
```

Exploring Additional Python Resources

As you continue your Python journey, you'll find a wealth of resources to help you learn and grow. Here are some valuable resources:

1. Official Documentation:

The official Python documentation (docs.python.org) is an essential resource for learning about Python's features, libraries, and modules.

2. Online Courses and Tutorials:

- **Codecademy**: Interactive Python courses that cover various topics from basics to advanced.
- **Coursera**: Offers courses from universities and institutions on Python programming and data science.
- **edX**: Provides Python courses from top universities and institutions.

3. **Books:**

- **"Automate the Boring Stuff with Python" by Al Sweigart**: A great book for beginners that teaches practical programming skills.
- **"Python Crash Course" by Eric Matthes**: A hands-on, project-based introduction to Python.
- **"Fluent Python" by Luciano Ramalho**: An in-depth guide for experienced programmers to write idiomatic Python code.

4. **Online Communities:**

- **Stack Overflow**: A Q&A platform where you can ask questions and get answers from the community.
- **Reddit**: Subreddits like r/learnpython and r/Python are great places to discuss Python-related topics.
- **Python Discord**: A community where you can chat with other Python developers.

Chapter 3: Essential Python Programming

Basic Syntax and Data Types

Python's simplicity and readability make it an excellent language for beginners and experienced programmers alike. In this chapter, we'll explore the fundamental aspects of Python, including its syntax, data types, and control structures.

1. Variables and Data Types:

In Python, variables are used to store data. You don't need to declare the variable type explicitly, as Python infers the type based on the value assigned.

– **Integer**: Whole numbers.

```
age = 30
```

– **Float**: Numbers with a decimal point.

```
height = 5.9
```

– **String**: A sequence of characters enclosed in quotes.

```
name = "Alice"
```

- **Boolean**: Represents `True` or `False`.

```
is_student = True
```

- **List**: An ordered collection of items.

```
fruits = ["apple", "banana", "cherry"]
```

- **Tuple**: An immutable ordered collection of items.

```
coordinates = (10.0, 20.0)
```

- **Set**: An unordered collection of unique items.

```
unique_numbers = {1, 2, 3, 4, 5}
```

- **Dictionary**: A collection of key-value pairs.

```
student = {"name": "Alice", "age": 25, "major": "Computer Science"}
```

2. Type Conversion:

You can convert between different data types using built-in functions.

```
age = "25"          # String
age_int = int(age)  # Convert to integer
height = 5.9
height_str = str(height)  # Convert to string
```

Control Structures

Control structures allow you to control the flow of your program. The primary control structures in Python are conditionals and loops.

1. Conditional Statements (if, elif, else):

Conditional statements execute different blocks of code based on certain conditions.

```
age = 20

if age >= 18:
    print("You are an adult.")
elif age >= 13:
    print("You are a teenager.")
else:
    print("You are a child.")
```

2. Loops (for, while):

Loops allow you to execute a block of code multiple times.

- **For Loop**: Used to iterate over a sequence (like a list, tuple, or string).

```
for fruit in ["apple", "banana", "cherry"]:
    print(fruit)
```

- **While Loop**: Repeats as long as a condition is true.

```
count = 0
while count < 5:
    print(count)
    count += 1
```

Functions and Modules

Functions and modules help you organize and reuse code. Functions are defined using the `def` keyword, while modules are collections of related functions and variables.

1. Defining and Calling Functions:

Functions encapsulate a block of code that can be reused.

```
def greet(name):
    print(f"Hello, {name}!")

greet("Alice")  # Outputs: Hello, Alice!
```

2. Function Arguments:

Functions can accept positional, keyword, and default arguments.

```
def add(a, b=5):
    return a + b

print(add(3))       # Outputs: 8 (3 + 5)
print(add(3, 2))    # Outputs: 5 (3 + 2)
```

3. Returning Values:
Functions can return values using the `return` statement.

```
def square(x):
    return x * x

result = square(4)   # result is 16
```

4. Lambda Functions:
Lambda functions are small anonymous functions defined with the `lambda` keyword.

```
square = lambda x: x * x
print(square(5))   # Outputs: 25
```

5. Modules and Packages:
Modules are files containing Python code (functions, classes, variables) that can be imported into other Python scripts. Packages are collections of modules.

- **Creating a Module**:

Create a file named mymodule.py:

```
def greet(name):
    return f"Hello, {name}!"
```

- **Importing a Module**:

```
import mymodule

print(mymodule.greet("Alice"))  # Outputs: Hello, Alice!
```

- **Using** from ... import ...:

```
from mymodule import greet

print(greet("Bob"))  # Outputs: Hello, Bob!
```

File Handling

Python provides built-in functions for file handling, allowing you to read from and write to files.

1. Reading Files:

```
with open("example.txt", "r") as file:
    content = file.read()
    print(content)
```

2. Writing to Files:

```
with open("example.txt", "w") as file:
    file.write("Hello, World!")
```

3. Appending to Files:

```
with open("example.txt", "a") as file:
    file.write("\nAppend this line.")
```

Exception Handling

Exception handling allows you to manage errors gracefully using `try`, `except`, `else`, and `finally` blocks.

```
try:
    result = 10 / 0
except ZeroDivisionError:
    print("Cannot divide by zero!")
else:
    print("Division successful!")
finally:
```

```
    print("This will always
execute.")
```

Object-Oriented Programming (OOP)

Python supports object-oriented programming (OOP) principles, allowing you to define classes and create objects.

1. Defining Classes and Creating Objects:

```
class Dog:
    def __init__(self, name, age):
        self.name = name
        self.age = age

    def bark(self):
        return f"{self.name} says woof!"

my_dog = Dog("Buddy", 3)
print(my_dog.bark())  # Outputs: Buddy says woof!
```

2. Inheritance:

Inheritance allows a class to inherit attributes and methods from another class.

```
class Animal:
    def __init__(self, name):
        self.name = name

    def speak(self):
```

```
        raise
NotImplementedError("Subclass must
implement abstract method")

class Cat(Animal):
    def speak(self):
        return f"{self.name} says
meow!"

my_cat = Cat("Whiskers")
print(my_cat.speak())  # Outputs:
Whiskers says meow!
```

3. Encapsulation:

Encapsulation restricts access to certain methods and variables, which can prevent the accidental modification of data.

```
class Car:
    def __init__(self, make, model):
        self._make = make
        self._model = model

    def get_make(self):
        return self._make

    def set_make(self, make):
        self._make = make

my_car = Car("Toyota", "Corolla")
```

```python
print(my_car.get_make())   # Outputs: Toyota
```

4. Polymorphism:

Polymorphism allows methods to be used interchangeably between different classes that implement the same interface.

```python
class Bird:
    def speak(self):
        return "Chirp!"

class Duck(Bird):
    def speak(self):
        return "Quack!"

class Parrot(Bird):
    def speak(self):
        return "Squawk!"

def make_bird_speak(bird):
    print(bird.speak())

duck = Duck()
parrot = Parrot()

make_bird_speak(duck)      # Outputs: Quack!
make_bird_speak(parrot)    # Outputs: Squawk!
```

Working with Collections

Python provides powerful built-in collections for storing and manipulating data.

1. Lists:
Lists are ordered, mutable collections of items.

```
fruits = ["apple", "banana", "cherry"]
fruits.append("date")
print(fruits)   # Outputs: ['apple', 'banana', 'cherry', 'date']
```

2. Tuples:
Tuples are ordered, immutable collections of items.

```
coordinates = (10.0, 20.0)
print(coordinates)   # Outputs: (10.0, 20.0)
```

3. Sets:
Sets are unordered collections of unique items.

```
unique_numbers = {1, 2, 3, 4, 5}
unique_numbers.add(6)
print(unique_numbers)   # Outputs: {1, 2, 3, 4, 5, 6}
```

4. Dictionaries:
Dictionaries are collections of key-value pairs.

```
student = {"name": "Alice", "age":
25, "major": "Computer Science"}
print(student["name"])   # Outputs:
Alice
```

5. List Comprehensions:

List comprehensions provide a concise way to create lists.

```
squares = [x**2 for x in range(10)]
print(squares)   # Outputs: [0, 1, 4,
9, 16, 25,

 36, 49, 64, 81]
```

6. Dictionary Comprehensions:

Dictionary comprehensions provide a concise way to create dictionaries.

```
squares = {x: x**2 for x in
range(10)}
print(squares)   # Outputs: {0: 0, 1:
1, 2: 4, 3: 9, 4: 16, 5: 25, 6: 36,
7: 49, 8: 64, 9: 81}
```

Regular Expressions

Regular expressions (regex) are patterns used to match character combinations in strings. The `re` module provides support for working with regular expressions.

1. Basic Pattern Matching:

```
import re

pattern = r"\b[a-zA-Z]{3}\b"  #
Matches any three-letter word
text = "The cat sat on the mat."

matches = re.findall(pattern, text)
print(matches)   # Outputs: ['cat',
'sat', 'the', 'mat']
```

2. Groups and Quantifiers:

Groups and quantifiers allow you to specify more complex patterns.

```
pattern = r"(\b\w+\b)"
text = "The quick brown fox jumps
over the lazy dog."

matches = re.findall(pattern, text)
print(matches)   # Outputs: ['The',
'quick', 'brown', 'fox', 'jumps',
'over', 'the', 'lazy', 'dog']
```

3. Substitution and Splitting:

You can use regex for substitution and splitting strings.

```
pattern = r"\s+"  # Matches any
whitespace sequence
text = "The quick brown fox"

# Substitution
```

```
replaced_text = re.sub(pattern, "-", 
text)
print(replaced_text)   # Outputs: The-
quick-brown-fox

# Splitting
split_text = re.split(pattern, text)
print(split_text)   # Outputs: ['The', 
'quick', 'brown', 'fox']
```

Working with Dates and Times

Python provides the `datetime` module for manipulating dates and times.

1. Getting the Current Date and Time:

```
from datetime import datetime

now = datetime.now()
print(now)   # Outputs the current 
date and time
```

2. Creating Specific Dates and Times:

```
from datetime import datetime

specific_date = datetime(2020, 5, 17)
print(specific_date)   # Outputs: 
2020-05-17 00:00:00
```

3. Formatting Dates and Times:

```
from datetime import datetime

now = datetime.now()
formatted_date = now.strftime("%Y-%m-%d %H:%M:%S")
print(formatted_date)  # Outputs: formatted current date and time
```

4. Parsing Strings into Dates:

```
from datetime import datetime

date_string = "2020-05-17 12:00:00"
parsed_date = datetime.strptime(date_string, "%Y-%m-%d %H:%M:%S")
print(parsed_date)  # Outputs: 2020-05-17 12:00:00
```

Chapter 4: Data Handling with Python

Introduction

Data handling is one of the most crucial skills for any programmer, especially those working in data science, analytics, and machine learning. Python provides a wide array of libraries and tools to facilitate efficient data handling. In this chapter, we will explore various methods to load, explore, manipulate, and save data using Python's powerful libraries, primarily focusing on Pandas.

Loading Data

Python can handle various data formats, such as CSV, Excel, JSON, and SQL databases. The Pandas library offers versatile functions to load data from these formats into DataFrames, a two-dimensional data structure with labeled axes.

1. Loading Data from CSV Files:

CSV (Comma-Separated Values) is one of the most common data formats. Pandas provides the `read_csv` function to load CSV files.

```
import pandas as pd

# Load CSV data into a DataFrame
df = pd.read_csv('data.csv')
```

```
print(df.head())    # Display the first
five rows of the DataFrame
```

2. Loading Data from Excel Files:

Excel is widely used for data storage and manipulation. Pandas can read Excel files using the `read_excel` function.

```
# Load Excel data into a DataFrame
df = pd.read_excel('data.xlsx',
sheet_name='Sheet1')
print(df.head())
```

3. Loading Data from JSON Files:

JSON (JavaScript Object Notation) is a lightweight data-interchange format. Pandas can read JSON files using the `read_json` function.

```
# Load JSON data into a DataFrame
df = pd.read_json('data.json')
print(df.head())
```

4. Loading Data from SQL Databases:

SQL databases are used to store and manage large datasets. Pandas can interact with SQL databases using the `read_sql` function.

```
import sqlite3

# Connect to the database
conn = sqlite3.connect('database.db')
```

```
# Load data from a SQL query into a
DataFrame
df = pd.read_sql('SELECT * FROM
table_name', conn)
print(df.head())
```

Exploring Data

Once the data is loaded into a DataFrame, the next step is to explore and understand its structure and contents. Pandas offers various functions for data exploration.

1. Displaying Basic Information:

- `head` **and** `tail` **Functions**: Display the first and last few rows of the DataFrame.

    ```
    print(df.head())    # First five rows
    print(df.tail())    # Last five rows
    ```

- `info` **Function**: Provides a summary of the DataFrame, including the number of non-null entries and data types.

    ```
    print(df.info())
    ```

- `describe` **Function**: Generates descriptive statistics of numerical columns.

```
print(df.describe())
```

2. Accessing Specific Data:

- **Accessing Columns**: Use the column name to access a specific column.

```
print(df['column_name'])
```

- **Accessing Rows**: Use the `iloc` and `loc` functions to access rows by index or label.

```
print(df.iloc[0])   # First row
print(df.loc[0])    # First row (if the index is labeled 0)
```

- **Filtering Data**: Use boolean indexing to filter data based on conditions.

```
filtered_df = df[df['column_name'] > 10]
print(filtered_df)
```

Data Manipulation

Data manipulation involves transforming data into a suitable format for analysis. Pandas provides powerful functions for various data manipulation tasks.

1. Handling Missing Data:

Missing data can cause issues in analysis and modeling. Pandas offers several methods to handle missing data.

- **Identifying Missing Data**: Use the `isnull` function to identify missing values.

    ```
    print(df.isnull().sum())
    ```

- **Filling Missing Data**: Use the `fillna` function to fill missing values with a specified value.

    ```
    df['column_name'].fillna(0, inplace=True)
    ```

- **Dropping Missing Data**: Use the `dropna` function to remove rows or columns with missing values.

    ```
    df.dropna(inplace=True)
    ```

2. Data Transformation:

Data transformation involves changing the structure or values of data to facilitate analysis.

- **Renaming Columns**: Use the `rename` function to rename columns.

    ```
    df.rename(columns={'old_name': 'new_name'}, inplace=True)
    ```

- **Applying Functions**: Use the `apply` function to apply a custom function to each element in a column.

    ```
    df['column_name'] = df['column_name'].apply(lambda x: x * 2)
    ```

- **Replacing Values**: Use the `replace` function to replace specific values.

    ```
    df['column_name'].replace('old_value', 'new_value', inplace=True)
    ```

3. Grouping and Aggregating Data:

Grouping and aggregating data are essential for summarizing and analyzing large datasets.

- **Grouping Data**: Use the `groupby` function to group data by one or more columns.

```
grouped_df =
df.groupby('group_column')
```

- **Aggregating Data**: Use aggregation functions like `sum`, `mean`, `count`, etc., on grouped data.

```
aggregated_df =
grouped_df['value_column'].sum()
print(aggregated_df)
```

4. Merging and Joining Data:
Combining data from multiple sources is a common task. Pandas provides functions for merging and joining DataFrames.

- **Merging DataFrames**: Use the `merge` function to combine DataFrames based on a common column.

```
merged_df = pd.merge(df1, df2,
on='common_column')
```

- **Joining DataFrames**: Use the `join` function to join DataFrames based on their index.

```
joined_df = df1.join(df2,
lsuffix='_left', rsuffix='_right')
```

5. Reshaping Data:

Reshaping data involves changing its structure without altering the actual data values.

- **Pivoting Data**: Use the `pivot` function to reshape data based on column values.

```
pivoted_df =
df.pivot(index='index_column',
columns='columns_column',
values='values_column')
```

- **Melting Data**: Use the `melt` function to unpivot data.

```
melted_df = pd.melt(df,
id_vars=['id_column'],
value_vars=['value_column'])
```

Data Visualisation

Data visualisation is a crucial step in data analysis, as it helps to uncover patterns, trends, and insights. Python provides powerful libraries for data visualisation, such as Matplotlib and Seaborn.

1. Introduction to Matplotlib:

Matplotlib is a widely used library for creating static, interactive, and animated plots in Python.

- **Basic Plotting**: Use the `plot` function to create line plots.

  ```
  import matplotlib.pyplot as plt

  plt.plot(df['x_column'], df['y_column'])
  plt.xlabel('X-axis Label')
  plt.ylabel('Y-axis Label')
  plt.title('Plot Title')
  plt.show()
  ```

- **Bar Plots**: Use the `bar` function to create bar plots.

  ```
  plt.bar(df['x_column'], df['y_column'])
  plt.xlabel('X-axis Label')
  plt.ylabel('Y-axis Label')
  plt.title('Bar Plot Title')
  plt.show()
  ```

- **Scatter Plots**: Use the `scatter` function to create scatter plots.

  ```
  plt.scatter(df['x_column'], df['y_column'])
  plt.xlabel('X-axis Label')
  ```

```
plt.ylabel('Y-axis Label')
plt.title('Scatter Plot Title')
plt.show()
```

2. Advanced Visualisation with Seaborn:

Seaborn is built on top of Matplotlib and provides a high-level interface for creating attractive and informative statistical graphics.

– **Distribution Plots**: Use the `distplot` function to visualise data distribution.

```
import seaborn as sns

sns.distplot(df['column_name'])
plt.title('Distribution Plot')
plt.show()
```

– **Box Plots**: Use the `boxplot` function to visualise data distribution across categories.

```
sns.boxplot(x='category_column',
y='value_column', data=df)
plt.title('Box Plot')
plt.show()
```

– **Heatmaps**: Use the `heatmap` function to visualise correlation matrices.

```
correlation_matrix = df.corr()
sns.heatmap(correlation_matrix,
annot=True)
plt.title('Heatmap')
plt.show()
```

Saving Data

After manipulating and analysing data, you may want to save the results. Pandas provides functions to save DataFrames in various formats.

1. Saving Data to CSV Files:
Use the `to_csv` function to save DataFrames to CSV files.

```
df.to_csv('output.csv', index=False)
```

2. Saving Data to Excel Files:
Use the `to_excel` function to save DataFrames to Excel files.

```
df.to_excel('output.xlsx',
index=False)
```

3. Saving Data to JSON Files:
Use the `to_json` function to save DataFrames to JSON files.

```
df.to_json('output.json')
```

4. Saving Data to SQL Databases:

Use the to_sql function to save DataFrames to SQL databases.

```
df.to_sql('table_name', conn,
if_exists='replace', index=False)
```

Practical Examples

To solidify your understanding of data handling with Python, let's walk through a practical example using a sample dataset. We'll perform data loading, exploration, manipulation, visualisation, and saving.

Example: Analysing Superstore Sales Data

1. **Loading the Data:**

```
import pandas as pd

# Load the dataset
df = pd.read_csv('superstore_sales.csv')
```

2. **Exploring the Data:**

```
# Display basic information
print(df.info())
```

```python
# Display descriptive statistics
print(df.describe())

# Display the first few rows
print(df.head())
```

3. **Handling Missing Data:**

```python
# Identify missing values
print(df.isnull().sum())

# Fill missing values with a placeholder
df.fillna('Unknown', inplace=True)
```

4. **Data Transformation:**

```python
# Rename columns
df.rename(columns={'Order Date': 'Order_Date', 'Ship Date': 'Ship_Date'}, inplace=True)

# Convert date columns to datetime
df['Order_Date'] = pd.to_datetime(df['Order_Date'])
```

```python
df['Ship_Date'] = 
pd.to_datetime(df['Ship_Date'])
```

5. **Grouping and Aggregating Data:**

```python
# Group by 'Category' and calculate
total sales
category_sales = 
df.groupby('Category')['Sales'].sum()
print(category_sales)
```

6. **Merging DataFrames:**

Assume we have another DataFrame with category discounts:

```python
discounts = pd.DataFrame({
    'Category': ['Furniture', 'Office 
Supplies', 'Technology'],
    'Discount': [0.1, 0.15, 0.2]
})

# Merge the DataFrames
merged_df = pd.merge(df, discounts, 
on='Category')
```

7. **Data Visualisation:**

```python
import matplotlib.pyplot as plt
```

```python
import seaborn as sns

# Bar plot of total sales by category
category_sales.plot(kind='bar')
plt.xlabel('Category')
plt.ylabel('Total Sales')
plt.title('Total Sales by Category')
plt.show()

# Distribution plot of sales
sns.distplot(df['Sales'])
plt.title('Sales Distribution')
plt.show()
```

8. **Saving the Results:**

```python
# Save the cleaned and transformed data to a new CSV file
df.to_csv('cleaned_superstore_sales.csv', index=False)
```

Chapter 5: Advanced Data Manipulation

Introduction

As you progress in your data handling journey, you'll encounter more complex tasks that require advanced data manipulation techniques. These techniques enable you to clean, transform, and prepare your data for analysis, ensuring it is in the optimal format for extracting insights. In this chapter, we will explore advanced data manipulation techniques using Python's Pandas library, covering topics such as handling missing data, advanced grouping and aggregation, merging and joining DataFrames, and reshaping data.

Handling Missing Data

Missing data is a common issue in real-world datasets. Properly handling missing data is crucial to ensure the accuracy and reliability of your analysis. Pandas provides several methods to identify, fill, and remove missing data.

1. Identifying Missing Data:

Use the `isnull` and `notnull` functions to identify missing values in a DataFrame.

```
import pandas as pd

# Sample DataFrame
```

```
data = {'A': [1, 2, None, 4, 5], 'B':
[5, None, None, 8, 9], 'C': [10, 11,
12, None, 14]}
df = pd.DataFrame(data)

# Identify missing values
print(df.isnull())
print(df.notnull())
```

2. Filling Missing Data:

- **Fill with a Specific Value**: Use the `fillna` function to fill missing values with a specified value.

    ```
    df_filled = df.fillna(0)
    print(df_filled)
    ```

- **Forward Fill**: Propagate the last valid observation forward to the next valid.

    ```
    df_ffill = df.fillna(method='ffill')
    print(df_ffill)
    ```

- **Backward Fill**: Propagate the next valid observation backward to the next valid.

    ```
    df_bfill = df.fillna(method='bfill')
    ```

```
print(df_bfill)
```

- **Fill with Mean, Median, or Mode**: Fill missing values with the mean, median, or mode of the column.

```
df_mean = df.fillna(df.mean())
df_median = df.fillna(df.median())
df_mode =
df.fillna(df.mode().iloc[0])
print(df_mean)
print(df_median)
print(df_mode)
```

3. **Dropping Missing Data:**

    - **Drop Rows with Missing Values**: Use the dropna function to remove rows with missing values.

    ```
    df_dropped_rows = df.dropna()
    print(df_dropped_rows)
    ```

    - **Drop Columns with Missing Values**: Remove columns with missing values.

    ```
    df_dropped_columns =
    df.dropna(axis=1)
    print(df_dropped_columns)
    ```

Advanced Grouping and Aggregation

Grouping and aggregating data are fundamental operations for summarizing and analyzing large datasets. Pandas provides powerful functions to perform these tasks.

1. Grouping Data:

Use the `groupby` function to group data by one or more columns.

```
# Sample DataFrame
data = {'Category': ['A', 'A', 'B',
'B', 'C'], 'Values': [10, 20, 30, 40,
50]}
df = pd.DataFrame(data)

# Group by 'Category'
grouped = df.groupby('Category')
print(grouped)
```

2. Aggregating Data:

Apply aggregation functions to the grouped data.

– **Sum**: Calculate the sum of each group.

```
sum_values = grouped['Values'].sum()
print(sum_values)
```

– **Mean**: Calculate the mean of each group.

```
mean_values =
grouped['Values'].mean()
print(mean_values)
```

- **Custom Aggregation**: Use the `agg` function to apply multiple aggregation functions.

```
agg_values =
grouped['Values'].agg(['sum', 'mean',
'count'])
print(agg_values)
```

3. Grouping by Multiple Columns:
You can group data by multiple columns by passing a list of column names to the `groupby` function.

```
# Sample DataFrame
data = {'Category': ['A', 'A', 'B',
'B', 'C'], 'Subcategory': ['X', 'Y',
'X', 'Y', 'X'], 'Values': [10, 20,
30, 40, 50]}
df = pd.DataFrame(data)

# Group by 'Category' and
'Subcategory'
grouped = df.groupby(['Category',
'Subcategory'])
agg_values =
grouped['Values'].agg(['sum',
'mean'])
```

```
print(agg_values)
```

4. Transforming Grouped Data:

Use the `transform` function to apply a function to each group and return a DataFrame with the same shape as the original.

```
# Subtract the mean of each group
from the original values
df['Transformed_Values'] =
grouped['Values'].transform(lambda x:
x - x.mean())
print(df)
```

Merging and Joining DataFrames

Combining data from multiple sources is often necessary in data analysis. Pandas provides functions for merging and joining DataFrames based on common columns or indices.

1. Merging DataFrames:

Use the `merge` function to combine DataFrames based on common columns.

```
# Sample DataFrames
df1 = pd.DataFrame({'ID': [1, 2, 3],
'Name': ['Alice', 'Bob', 'Charlie']})
df2 = pd.DataFrame({'ID': [1, 2, 4],
'Score': [85, 90, 95]})

# Merge DataFrames on 'ID'
```

```
merged_df = pd.merge(df1, df2,
on='ID')
print(merged_df)
```

2. Types of Joins:

Specify the type of join using the how parameter in the merge function.

- **Inner Join**: Default join type, returns rows with matching keys in both DataFrames.

    ```
    inner_join = pd.merge(df1, df2,
    on='ID', how='inner')
    print(inner_join)
    ```

- **Left Join**: Returns all rows from the left DataFrame and matched rows from the right DataFrame.

    ```
    left_join = pd.merge(df1, df2,
    on='ID', how='left')
    print(left_join)
    ```

- **Right Join**: Returns all rows from the right DataFrame and matched rows from the left DataFrame.

    ```
    right_join = pd.merge(df1, df2,
    on='ID', how='right')
    ```

```
print(right_join)
```

– **Outer Join**: Returns all rows when there is a match in either left or right DataFrame.

```
outer_join = pd.merge(df1, df2,
on='ID', how='outer')
print(outer_join)
```

3. Joining DataFrames:

Use the `join` function to join DataFrames based on their indices.

```
# Sample DataFrames
df1 = pd.DataFrame({'Name': ['Alice',
'Bob', 'Charlie']}, index=[1, 2, 3])
df2 = pd.DataFrame({'Score': [85, 90,
95]}, index=[1, 2, 4])

# Join DataFrames on their indices
joined_df = df1.join(df2,
how='inner')
print(joined_df)
```

4. Concatenating DataFrames:

Use the `concat` function to concatenate DataFrames along a particular axis.

```
# Sample DataFrames
df1 = pd.DataFrame({'A': [1, 2, 3]})
```

```python
df2 = pd.DataFrame({'B': [4, 5, 6]})

# Concatenate DataFrames along columns
concat_df = pd.concat([df1, df2], axis=1)
print(concat_df)

# Concatenate DataFrames along rows
concat_df = pd.concat([df1, df2], axis=0)
print(concat_df)
```

Reshaping Data

Reshaping data involves changing its structure without altering the actual data values. Pandas provides functions for pivoting and melting DataFrames.

1. Pivoting Data:

Use the `pivot` function to reshape data based on column values.

```python
# Sample DataFrame
data = {'Date': ['2021-01-01', '2021-01-01', '2021-01-02', '2021-01-02'], 'City': ['NY', 'LA', 'NY', 'LA'], 'Temperature': [30, 25, 32, 28]}
df = pd.DataFrame(data)

# Pivot DataFrame
```

```python
pivot_df = df.pivot(index='Date',
columns='City', values='Temperature')
print(pivot_df)
```

2. Pivot Tables:

Use the `pivot_table` function to create pivot tables with aggregation.

```python
# Sample DataFrame
data = {'Date': ['2021-01-01',
'2021-01-01', '2021-01-02',
'2021-01-02'], 'City': ['NY', 'LA',
'NY', 'LA'], 'Sales': [200, 150,

220, 180]}
df = pd.DataFrame(data)

# Create pivot table
pivot_table_df = pd.pivot_table(df,
values='Sales', index='Date',
columns='City', aggfunc='sum')
print(pivot_table_df)
```

3. Melting Data:

Use the `melt` function to unpivot data, transforming it from wide format to long format.

```python
# Sample DataFrame
data = {'ID': [1, 2, 3], 'Math': [90,
80, 85], 'Science': [85, 95, 80]}
df = pd.DataFrame(data)
```

```
# Melt DataFrame
melted_df = pd.melt(df,
id_vars=['ID'], value_vars=['Math',
'Science'], var_name='Subject',
value_name='Score')
print(melted_df)
```

4. Stacking and Unstacking:

Stacking and unstacking allow you to convert between long and wide formats.

- **Stacking**: Pivot the columns of a DataFrame into the index.

    ```
    stacked_df =
    df.set_index('ID').stack()
    print(stacked_df)
    ```

- **Unstacking**: Pivot the index of a DataFrame into columns.

    ```
    unstacked_df = stacked_df.unstack()
    print(unstacked_df)
    ```

Advanced Data Cleaning

Data cleaning is a critical step in data preparation. It involves identifying and correcting inaccuracies, inconsistencies, and other issues in the dataset.

1. Removing Duplicates:

Use the `drop_duplicates` function to remove duplicate rows.

```
# Sample DataFrame
data = {'A': [1, 2, 2, 3, 4, 4], 'B': [5, 6, 6, 7, 8, 8]}
df = pd.DataFrame(data)

# Remove duplicate rows
df_cleaned = df.drop_duplicates()
print(df_cleaned)
```

2. Detecting Outliers:

Outliers can skew analysis results. Use statistical methods to detect outliers.

- **Using Z-Score**: Detect outliers based on the standard deviation.

```
from scipy import stats

df['Z_Score'] = stats.zscore(df['A'])
outliers = df[df['Z_Score'].abs() > 3]
```

```
print(outliers)
```

- **Using IQR (Interquartile Range)**: Detect outliers based on the interquartile range.

```
Q1 = df['A'].quantile(0.25)
Q3 = df['A'].quantile(0.75)
IQR = Q3 - Q1

outliers = df[(df['A'] < (Q1 - 1.5 * IQR)) | (df['A'] > (Q3 + 1.5 * IQR))]
print(outliers)
```

3. **Data Type Conversion:**
Ensure that columns have the correct data type for analysis.

```
# Convert column to numeric
df['A'] = pd.to_numeric(df['A'], errors='coerce')

# Convert column to datetime
df['Date'] = pd.to_datetime(df['Date'], errors='coerce')
```

4. **String Manipulation:**
Clean and transform string data using string methods.

- **Removing Whitespace**: Use the `strip` function to remove leading and trailing whitespace.

    ```
    df['Name'] = df['Name'].str.strip()
    ```

- **Replacing Substrings**: Use the `replace` function to replace substrings.

    ```
    df['Address'] =
    df['Address'].str.replace('Street',
    'St.')
    ```

- **Splitting Strings**: Use the `split` function to split strings into multiple columns.

    ```
    df[['First_Name', 'Last_Name']] =
    df['Full_Name'].str.split(' ',
    expand=True)
    ```

Practical Examples

To solidify your understanding of advanced data manipulation with Python, let's walk through a practical example using a sample dataset. We'll perform data cleaning, transformation, grouping, aggregation, merging, and reshaping.

Example: Analysing Retail Store Data

1. **Loading the Data:**

   ```
   import pandas as pd

   # Load the dataset
   df = pd.read_csv('retail_data.csv')
   ```

2. **Exploring the Data:**

   ```
   # Display basic information
   print(df.info())

   # Display descriptive statistics
   print(df.describe())

   # Display the first few rows
   print(df.head())
   ```

3. **Handling Missing Data:**

   ```
   # Identify missing values
   print(df.isnull().sum())

   # Fill missing values with the mean
   ```

```
df['Sales'] =
df['Sales'].fillna(df['Sales'].mean()
)
```

4. **Data Transformation:**

```
# Convert 'Date' column to datetime
df['Date'] =
pd.to_datetime(df['Date'])

# Create a new column for year
df['Year'] = df['Date'].dt.year

# Rename columns
df.rename(columns={'Product
Category': 'Category'}, inplace=True)
```

5. **Grouping and Aggregating Data:**

```
# Group by 'Year' and calculate total
sales
yearly_sales = df.groupby('Year')
['Sales'].sum()
print(yearly_sales)
```

6. **Merging DataFrames:**

Assume we have another DataFrame with product information:

```
# Sample DataFrame
product_info = pd.DataFrame({'Product ID': [1, 2, 3], 'Category': ['Electronics', 'Furniture', 'Office Supplies']})

# Merge DataFrames on 'Category'
merged_df = pd.merge(df, product_info, on='Category')
print(merged_df.head())
```

7. **Reshaping Data:**

```
# Pivot table of total sales by year and category
pivot_table_df = pd.pivot_table(df, values='Sales', index='Year', columns='Category', aggfunc='sum')
print(pivot_table_df)
```

8. **Advanced Data Cleaning:**

```
# Remove duplicate rows
df_cleaned = df.drop_duplicates()
```

```
# Detect and remove outliers based on
IQR
Q1 =
df_cleaned['Sales'].quantile(0.25)
Q3 =
df_cleaned['Sales'].quantile(0.75)
IQR = Q3 - Q1

df_cleaned =
df_cleaned[(df_cleaned['Sales'] >=
(Q1 - 1.5 * IQR)) &
(df_cleaned['Sales'] <= (Q3 + 1.5 *
IQR))]
```

Conclusion

In this chapter, we delved into advanced data manipulation techniques using Python's Pandas library. We covered handling missing data, advanced grouping and aggregation, merging and joining DataFrames, reshaping data, and advanced data cleaning. Mastering these techniques is essential for preparing data for analysis and ensuring its quality and integrity. By practicing these methods on real-world datasets, you'll be well-equipped to handle complex data manipulation tasks and derive meaningful insights from your data.

Chapter 6: Data Visualisation

Introduction

Data visualisation is a powerful technique used to explore and communicate data insights effectively. By transforming data into visual representations, you can identify patterns, trends, and outliers that might not be apparent from raw data. Python provides several libraries for creating a wide range of visualisations, with Matplotlib and Seaborn being the most popular.

In this chapter, we will delve into the essentials of data visualisation using these libraries, covering various types of plots, customisation techniques, and practical examples.

Getting Started with Matplotlib

Matplotlib is a versatile library for creating static, animated, and interactive plots in Python. It is the foundation of many other visualisation libraries, including Seaborn.

1. Installing Matplotlib:

If you don't already have Matplotlib installed, you can install it using pip:

```
pip install matplotlib
```

2. Basic Plotting:

Let's start with a simple line plot.

```python
import matplotlib.pyplot as plt

# Sample data
x = [1, 2, 3, 4, 5]
y = [2, 3, 5, 7, 11]

# Create a line plot
plt.plot(x, y)
plt.xlabel('X-axis')
plt.ylabel('Y-axis')
plt.title('Simple Line Plot')
plt.show()
```

This code generates a basic line plot with labeled axes and a title.

Types of Plots

Matplotlib supports various types of plots to visualise different kinds of data. Here are some commonly used plots:

1. Line Plot:

Line plots are useful for visualising trends over time.

```python
# Sample data
years = [2015, 2016, 2017, 2018, 2019, 2020]
values = [100, 200, 300, 400, 500, 600]

# Create a line plot
plt.plot(years, values, marker='o')
plt.xlabel('Year')
```

```
plt.ylabel('Value')
plt.title('Line Plot Example')
plt.grid(True)
plt.show()
```

2. Bar Plot:

Bar plots are useful for comparing quantities across categories.

```
# Sample data
categories = ['A', 'B', 'C', 'D']
values = [4, 7, 1, 8]

# Create a bar plot
plt.bar(categories, values, color='skyblue')
plt.xlabel('Category')
plt.ylabel('Value')
plt.title('Bar Plot Example')
plt.show()
```

3. Histogram:

Histograms are useful for visualising the distribution of a dataset.

```
import numpy as np

# Sample data
data = np.random.randn(1000)

# Create a histogram
```

```python
plt.hist(data, bins=30,
edgecolor='black')
plt.xlabel('Value')
plt.ylabel('Frequency')
plt.title('Histogram Example')
plt.show()
```

4. Scatter Plot:

Scatter plots are useful for visualising the relationship between two variables.

```python
# Sample data
x = np.random.randn(100)
y = np.random.randn(100)

# Create a scatter plot
plt.scatter(x, y, alpha=0.5,
color='purple')
plt.xlabel('X-axis')
plt.ylabel('Y-axis')
plt.title('Scatter Plot Example')
plt.show()
```

5. Pie Chart:

Pie charts are useful for visualizing the composition of a dataset.

```python
# Sample data
sizes = [15, 30, 45, 10]
labels = ['A', 'B', 'C', 'D']
```

```python
# Create a pie chart
plt.pie(sizes, labels=labels,
autopct='%1.1f%%', startangle=90)
plt.title('Pie Chart Example')
plt.show()
```

Customising Plots

Customisation is key to making your plots informative and visually appealing. Matplotlib provides extensive options for customising plots.

1. Adding Legends:
Legends help identify different data series in a plot.

```python
# Sample data
x = np.linspace(0, 10, 100)
y1 = np.sin(x)
y2 = np.cos(x)

# Create line plots
plt.plot(x, y1, label='Sine')
plt.plot(x, y2, label='Cosine')
plt.xlabel('X-axis')
plt.ylabel('Y-axis')
plt.title('Plot with Legend')
plt.legend()
plt.show()
```

2. Customizing Line Styles and Colors:
You can customize line styles, colors, and markers to enhance your plots.

```python
# Create customized line plots
plt.plot(x, y1, linestyle='--',
color='red', marker='o',
label='Sine')
plt.plot(x, y2, linestyle='-',
color='blue', marker='x',
label='Cosine')
plt.xlabel('X-axis')
plt.ylabel('Y-axis')
plt.title('Customized Line Plot')
plt.legend()
plt.show()
```

3. Adding Annotations:

Annotations help highlight specific points or areas in a plot.

```python
# Create a line plot
plt.plot(x, y1, label='Sine')
plt.xlabel('X-axis')
plt.ylabel('Y-axis')
plt.title('Plot with Annotation')
plt.legend()

# Add annotation
plt.annotate('Max value', xy=(np.pi/
2, 1), xytext=(np.pi/2 + 1, 1.5),

arrowprops=dict(facecolor='black',
shrink=0.05))
plt.show()
```

4. Adjusting Plot Size and Layout:

You can adjust the size and layout of your plots to make them fit better in your reports or presentations.

```
# Create a line plot with custom size
plt.figure(figsize=(10, 6))
plt.plot(x, y1, label='Sine')
plt.xlabel('X-axis')
plt.ylabel('Y-axis')
plt.title('Custom Size Plot')
plt.legend()
plt.tight_layout()
plt.show()
```

Advanced Visualisation with Seaborn

Seaborn is built on top of Matplotlib and provides a high-level interface for creating attractive and informative statistical graphics. It is particularly well-suited for visualising complex datasets.

1. Installing Seaborn:

If you don't already have Seaborn installed, you can install it using pip:

```
pip install seaborn
```

2. Basic Seaborn Plotting:

Seaborn simplifies the creation of many types of plots.

```
import seaborn as sns
```

```
# Sample data
tips = sns.load_dataset('tips')

# Create a scatter plot
sns.scatterplot(data=tips,
x='total_bill', y='tip')
plt.title('Scatter Plot with
Seaborn')
plt.show()
```

3. Distribution Plots:

Seaborn provides several functions for visualising the distribution of a dataset.

– **Histogram**:

```
sns.histplot(data=tips,
x='total_bill', kde=True)
plt.title('Histogram with KDE')
plt.show()
```

– **Box Plot**:

Box plots are useful for visualising the distribution and identifying outliers.

```
sns.boxplot(data=tips, x='day',
y='total_bill')
plt.title('Box Plot Example')
```

```
plt.show()
```

– **Violin Plot:**

Violin plots combine aspects of box plots and KDE.

```
sns.violinplot(data=tips, x='day',
y='total_bill')
plt.title('Violin Plot Example')
plt.show()
```

4. Pair Plot:
Pair plots are useful for visualising pairwise relationships in a dataset.

```
sns.pairplot(tips)
plt.title('Pair Plot Example')
plt.show()
```

5. Heatmaps:
Heatmaps are useful for visualising the correlation matrix of a dataset.

```
# Calculate the correlation matrix
correlation_matrix = tips.corr()

# Create a heatmap
sns.heatmap(correlation_matrix,
annot=True, cmap='coolwarm')
plt.title('Heatmap Example')
```

```
plt.show()
```

6. Facet Grids:

Facet grids are useful for visualising the distribution of a dataset across multiple subsets.

```
# Create a facet grid of histograms
g = sns.FacetGrid(tips, col='day',
height=4, aspect=0.7)
g.map(sns.histplot, 'total_bill')
plt.show()
```

Interactive Visualisations with Plotly

Plotly is a powerful library for creating interactive visualisations. It supports a wide range of chart types and allows for complex interactions.

1. Installing Plotly:

If you don't already have Plotly installed, you can install it using pip:

```
pip install plotly
```

2. Basic Plotly Plotting:

Let's create a simple interactive line plot using Plotly.

```
import plotly.graph_objs as go
import plotly.offline as pyo

# Sample data
x = [1, 2, 3, 4, 5]
```

```
y = [2, 3, 5, 7, 11]

# Create a line plot
trace = go.Scatter(x=x, y=y,
mode='lines+markers', name='Data')
layout = go.Layout(title='Interactive
Line Plot', xaxis=dict(title='X-
axis'), yaxis=dict(title='Y-axis'))
fig = go.Figure(data=[trace],
layout=layout)
pyo.plot(fig)
```

3. Advanced Plotly Visualisations:

Plotly supports many advanced visualisations, including 3D plots and geographic maps.

– **3D Scatter Plot**:

```
# Sample data
z = [10, 20, 30, 40, 50]

# Create a 3D scatter plot
trace = go.Scatter3d(x=x, y=y, z=z,
mode='markers', marker=dict(size=5,
color=z, colorscale='Viridis'))
layout = go.Layout(title='3D Scatter
Plot')
fig = go.Figure(data=[trace],
layout=layout)
```

```
pyo.plot(fig)
```

- **Choropleth Map**:

Choropleth maps are useful for visualising data across geographic areas.

```
import plotly.express as px

# Sample data
df = px.data.gapminder().query("year == 2007")

# Create a choropleth map
fig = px.choropleth(df,
locations="iso_alpha",
color="lifeExp",
hover_name="country",
color_continuous_scale=px.colors.sequential.Plasma)
fig.update_layout(title='Choropleth Map')
fig.show()
```

Practical Examples

To solidify your understanding of data visualisation with Python, let's walk through practical examples using sample datasets.

Example 1: Visualising Sales Data

1. Loading the Data:

```
import pandas as pd

# Load the dataset
df = pd.read_csv('sales_data.csv')
```

2. Exploring the Data:

```
# Display basic information
print(df.info())

# Display descriptive statistics
print(df.describe())

# Display the first few rows
print(df.head())
```

3. Creating Visualisations:

– Line Plot of Monthly Sales:

```
df['Date'] = pd.to_datetime(df['Date'])
df.set_index('Date', inplace=True)
```

```
monthly_sales = 
df['Sales'].resample('M').sum()

plt.figure(figsize=(10, 6))
plt.plot(monthly_sales, marker='o')
plt.xlabel('Date')
plt.ylabel('Sales')
plt.title('Monthly Sales')
plt.grid(True)
plt.show()
```

– **Bar Plot of Sales by Product Category**:

```
category_sales = 
df.groupby('Category')['Sales'].sum()

plt.figure(figsize=(10, 6))
category_sales.plot(kind='bar', 
color='skyblue')
plt.xlabel('Category')
plt.ylabel('Sales')
plt.title('Sales by Product 
Category')
plt.show()
```

– **Heatmap of Correlation Matrix:**

```
correlation_matrix = df.corr()
```

```
plt.figure(figsize=(10, 6))
sns.heatmap(correlation_matrix,
annot=True, cmap='coolwarm')
plt.title('Correlation Matrix
Heatmap')
plt.show()
```

Example 2: Visualising Titanic Dataset

1. **Loading the Data:**

```
# Load the Titanic dataset
titanic = sns.load_dataset('titanic')
```

2. **Exploring the Data:**

```
# Display basic information
print(titanic.info())

# Display descriptive statistics
print(titanic.describe())

# Display the first few rows
print(titanic.head())
```

3. **Creating Visualisations:**

– **Bar Plot of Survival Rate by Class:**

```
plt.figure(figsize=(10, 6))
sns.barplot(data=titanic, x='class',
y='survived', ci=None)
plt.xlabel('Class')
plt.ylabel('Survival Rate')
plt.title('Survival Rate by Class')
plt.show()
```

– **Box Plot of Age Distribution by Class:**

```
plt.figure(figsize=(10, 6))
sns.boxplot(data=titanic, x='class',
y='age')
plt.xlabel('Class')
plt.ylabel('Age')
plt.title('Age Distribution by
Class')
plt.show()
```

– **Pair Plot of Selected Features:**

```
selected_features = ['age', 'fare',
'survived']
sns.pairplot(titanic[selected_feature
s], hue='survived')
```

```
plt.suptitle('Pair Plot of Selected
Features', y=1.02)
plt.show()
```

Conclusion

In this chapter, we explored the essentials of data visualisation using Python's Matplotlib, Seaborn, and Plotly libraries. We covered various types of plots, customisation techniques, and practical examples to help you create informative and visually appealing visualisations. Mastering these tools will enable you to effectively communicate data insights and make data-driven decisions. As you continue to practice and explore these techniques, you'll find that Python offers a robust and flexible environment for creating a wide range of visualisations.

Chapter 7: Statistical Analysis with Python

Introduction

Statistical analysis is a critical component of data science, enabling you to make sense of your data and derive meaningful insights. Python provides several powerful libraries for statistical analysis, including NumPy, SciPy, Pandas, and Statsmodels. In this chapter, we will explore how to perform various statistical analyses using these libraries, covering descriptive statistics, inferential statistics, hypothesis testing, regression analysis, and more.

Descriptive Statistics

Descriptive statistics summarise and describe the main features of a dataset. They provide a simple summary of the sample and measures such as mean, median, mode, standard deviation, and variance.

1. Basic Descriptive Statistics:
Use Pandas to calculate basic descriptive statistics.

```
import pandas as pd

# Sample DataFrame
data = {'A': [1, 2, 2, 3, 4], 'B': [5, 6, 7, 8, 9]}
df = pd.DataFrame(data)
```

```
# Calculate basic descriptive
statistics
print(df.describe())
```

2. Measures of Central Tendency:
Calculate the mean, median, and mode using Pandas and SciPy.

```
import numpy as np
from scipy import stats

# Mean
mean_A = df['A'].mean()
print(f"Mean of A: {mean_A}")

# Median
median_A = df['A'].median()
print(f"Median of A: {median_A}")

# Mode
mode_A = stats.mode(df['A'])
print(f"Mode of A: {mode_A.mode[0]}")
```

3. Measures of Dispersion:
Calculate the standard deviation, variance, and range.

```
# Standard Deviation
std_A = df['A'].std()
print(f"Standard Deviation of A: {std_A}")
```

```
# Variance
var_A = df['A'].var()
print(f"Variance of A: {var_A}")

# Range
range_A = df['A'].max() - df['A'].min()
print(f"Range of A: {range_A}")
```

4. Measures of Position:

Calculate the percentiles and interquartile range (IQR).

```
# Percentiles
percentiles_A = np.percentile(df['A'], [25, 50, 75])
print(f"25th, 50th, 75th percentiles of A: {percentiles_A}")

# Interquartile Range (IQR)
iqr_A = stats.iqr(df['A'])
print(f"IQR of A: {iqr_A}")
```

Inferential Statistics

Inferential statistics allow you to make inferences and predictions about a population based on a sample of data. This involves estimating population parameters, testing hypotheses, and making predictions.

1. Sampling and Estimation:

Sampling involves selecting a subset of data from a population to make inferences about the entire population.

Estimation involves determining population parameters from the sample.

- **Random Sampling**: Select a random sample from a DataFrame.

```
# Random sample of 3 rows
sample_df = df.sample(n=3)
print(sample_df)
```

- **Estimating Population Mean**: Use the sample mean to estimate the population mean.

```
sample_mean = sample_df['A'].mean()
print(f"Sample Mean of A: {sample_mean}")
```

2. Confidence Intervals:

A confidence interval provides a range of values within which the true population parameter is likely to fall.

```
import statsmodels.api as sm

# Calculate the 95% confidence
interval for the mean of column A
conf_interval = 
sm.stats.DescrStatsW(df['A']).tconfin
t_mean()
```

```
print(f"95% Confidence Interval for
the mean of A: {conf_interval}")
```

3. Hypothesis Testing:

Hypothesis testing involves making an assumption (the null hypothesis) and testing whether the data supports it. Common tests include t-tests, chi-square tests, and ANOVA.

- **One-Sample T-Test**: Test if the sample mean is significantly different from a known value.

```
from scipy import stats

# Null hypothesis: mean of A is 3
t_stat, p_value =
stats.ttest_1samp(df['A'], 3)
print(f"T-Statistic: {t_stat}, P-
Value: {p_value}")
```

- **Two-Sample T-Test**: Test if the means of two independent samples are significantly different.

```
# Sample DataFrame with two groups
data = {'Group': ['A', 'A', 'A', 'B',
'B', 'B'], 'Value': [1, 2, 3, 4, 5,
6]}
df = pd.DataFrame(data)

# Two-sample t-test
```

```
group_A = df[df['Group'] == 'A']
['Value']
group_B = df[df['Group'] == 'B']
['Value']
t_stat, p_value =
stats.ttest_ind(group_A, group_B)
print(f"T-Statistic: {t_stat}, P-
Value: {p_value}")
```

- **Paired T-Test**: Test if the means of two related samples are significantly different.

```
# Sample DataFrame with paired data
data = {'Before': [1, 2, 3, 4, 5],
'After': [2, 3, 4, 5, 6]}
df = pd.DataFrame(data)

# Paired t-test
t_stat, p_value =
stats.ttest_rel(df['Before'],
df['After'])
print(f"T-Statistic: {t_stat}, P-
Value: {p_value}")
```

- **Chi-Square Test**: Test if there is a significant association between two categorical variables.

```python
from scipy.stats import chi2_contingency

# Sample DataFrame with categorical data
data = {'A': ['Yes', 'No', 'Yes', 'No', 'Yes'], 'B': ['No', 'No', 'Yes', 'Yes', 'No']}
df = pd.DataFrame(data)

# Contingency table
contingency_table = pd.crosstab(df['A'], df['B'])

# Chi-square test
chi2, p, dof, expected = chi2_contingency(contingency_table)
print(f"Chi-Square: {chi2}, P-Value: {p}")
```

- **ANOVA (Analysis of Variance)**: Test if there are significant differences between the means of three or more groups.

```python
# Sample DataFrame with three groups
data = {'Group': ['A', 'A', 'A', 'B', 'B', 'B', 'C', 'C', 'C'], 'Value': [1, 2, 3, 4, 5, 6, 7, 8, 9]}
df = pd.DataFrame(data)
```

```
# ANOVA test
anova_result =
stats.f_oneway(df[df['Group'] == 'A']
['Value'],

df[df['Group'] == 'B']['Value'],

df[df['Group'] == 'C']['Value'])
print(f"F-Statistic:
{anova_result.statistic}, P-Value:
{anova_result.pvalue}")
```

Correlation and Regression Analysis

Correlation and regression analysis are used to examine the relationship between variables. Correlation measures the strength and direction of the relationship, while regression analysis models the relationship.

1. Correlation:

Calculate the correlation coefficient to measure the strength and direction of the relationship between two variables.

```
# Sample DataFrame
data = {'X': [1, 2, 3, 4, 5], 'Y':
[2, 4, 5, 4, 5]}
df = pd.DataFrame(data)

# Calculate correlation coefficient
correlation = df['X'].corr(df['Y'])
```

```python
print(f"Correlation Coefficient: {correlation}")

# Calculate correlation matrix
correlation_matrix = df.corr()
print(correlation_matrix)
```

2. Linear Regression:

Linear regression models the relationship between a dependent variable and one or more independent variables.

- **Simple Linear Regression**:

```python
import statsmodels.api as sm

# Sample DataFrame
data = {'X': [1, 2, 3, 4, 5], 'Y': [2, 4, 5, 4, 5]}
df = pd.DataFrame(data)

# Define dependent and independent variables
X = df['X']
Y = df['Y']

# Add a constant to the independent variable
X = sm.add_constant(X)

# Fit the linear regression model
```

```
model = sm.OLS(Y, X).fit()

# Print the model summary
print(model.summary())
```

– **Multiple Linear Regression**:

```
# Sample DataFrame
data = {'X1': [1, 2, 3, 4, 5], 'X2':
[2, 3, 4, 5, 6], 'Y': [2, 4, 5, 4,
5]}
df = pd.DataFrame(data)

# Define dependent and independent
variables
X

= df[['X1', 'X2']]
Y = df['Y']

# Add a constant to the independent
variables
X = sm.add_constant(X)

# Fit the linear regression model
model = sm.OLS(Y, X).fit()

# Print the model summary
print(model.summary())
```

3. Logistic Regression:

Logistic regression models the relationship between a binary dependent variable and one or more independent variables.

```
import statsmodels.api as sm

# Sample DataFrame
data = {'X1': [1, 2, 3, 4, 5], 'X2':
[2, 3, 4, 5, 6], 'Y': [0, 0, 1, 1,
1]}
df = pd.DataFrame(data)

# Define dependent and independent
variables
X = df[['X1', 'X2']]
Y = df['Y']

# Add a constant to the independent
variables
X = sm.add_constant(X)

# Fit the logistic regression model
model = sm.Logit(Y, X).fit()

# Print the model summary
print(model.summary())
```

Time Series Analysis

Time series analysis involves analysing data points collected or recorded at specific time intervals. Python provides powerful tools for time series analysis.

1. Time Series Decomposition:

Decompose a time series into trend, seasonal, and residual components.

```
import pandas as pd
import statsmodels.api as sm

# Sample time series data
data = {'Date':
pd.date_range(start='2021-01-01',
periods=12, freq='M'), 'Value': [112,
118, 132, 129, 121, 135, 148, 148,
136, 119, 104, 118]}
df = pd.DataFrame(data)
df.set_index('Date', inplace=True)

# Decompose the time series
decomposition =
sm.tsa.seasonal_decompose(df['Value']
, model='additive')
decomposition.plot()
plt.show()
```

2. Moving Averages:

Calculate moving averages to smooth out short-term fluctuations and highlight longer-term trends.

```python
# Calculate the rolling mean (moving
average)
df['Rolling_Mean'] =
df['Value'].rolling(window=3).mean()

# Plot the original data and the
rolling mean
plt.plot(df['Value'],
label='Original')
plt.plot(df['Rolling_Mean'],
label='Rolling Mean')
plt.legend()
plt.show()
```

3. Autocorrelation and Partial Autocorrelation:

Analyse the autocorrelation and partial autocorrelation of a time series.

```python
from statsmodels.graphics.tsaplots
import plot_acf, plot_pacf

# Plot autocorrelation function (ACF)
plot_acf(df['Value'])
plt.show()

# Plot partial autocorrelation
function (PACF)
plot_pacf(df['Value'])
plt.show()
```

4. ARIMA (AutoRegressive Integrated Moving Average):

Fit an ARIMA model to a time series.

```
from statsmodels.tsa.arima.model
import ARIMA

# Fit the ARIMA model
model = ARIMA(df['Value'], order=(1,
1, 1))
model_fit = model.fit()

# Print the model summary
print(model_fit.summary())

# Plot the original data and the
fitted values
plt.plot(df['Value'],
label='Original')
plt.plot(model_fit.fittedvalues,
label='Fitted')
plt.legend()
plt.show()
```

Advanced Statistical Techniques

Beyond basic statistical analysis, Python offers advanced techniques for specialised analyses.

1. Principal Component Analysis (PCA):

PCA reduces the dimensionality of data while retaining most of the variance.

```
from sklearn.decomposition import PCA
```

```python
# Sample DataFrame
data = {'X1': [1, 2, 3, 4, 5], 'X2':
[2, 3, 4, 5, 6], 'X3': [3, 4, 5, 6,
7]}
df = pd.DataFrame(data)

# Fit PCA
pca = PCA(n_components=2)
principal_components =
pca.fit_transform(df)

# Create a DataFrame with the
principal components
pca_df =
pd.DataFrame(principal_components,
columns=['PC1', 'PC2'])
print(pca_df)
```

2. Clustering:

Clustering groups data points into clusters based on similarity.

- **K-Means Clustering**:

```python
from sklearn.cluster import KMeans

# Sample DataFrame
data = {'X1': [1, 2, 3, 4, 5], 'X2':
[2, 3, 4, 5, 6]}
```

```
df = pd.DataFrame(data)

# Fit K-Means clustering
kmeans = KMeans(n_clusters=2, random_state=0).fit(df)

# Add cluster labels to the DataFrame
df['Cluster'] = kmeans.labels_
print(df)
```

– **Hierarchical Clustering**:

```
from scipy.cluster.hierarchy import dendrogram, linkage

# Sample DataFrame
data = {'X1': [1, 2, 3, 4, 5], 'X2': [2, 3, 4, 5, 6]}
df = pd.DataFrame(data)

# Perform hierarchical clustering
linked = linkage(df, method='ward')

# Plot the dendrogram
dendrogram(linked)
plt.show()
```

Practical Examples

To solidify your understanding of statistical analysis with Python, let's walk through practical examples using sample datasets.

Example 1: Analysing Exam Scores

1. **Loading the Data:**

```
# Sample DataFrame
data = {'Math': [85, 89, 92, 78, 88],
'Science': [90, 87, 85, 82, 90]}
df = pd.DataFrame(data)
```

2. **Descriptive Statistics:**

```
# Calculate basic descriptive statistics
print(df.describe())

# Calculate the mean, median, and mode
mean_math = df['Math'].mean()
median_math = df['Math'].median()
mode_math = stats.mode(df['Math']).mode[0]

print(f"Mean Math Score: {mean_math}")
```

```
print(f"Median Math Score:
{median_math}")
print(f"Mode Math Score:
{mode_math}")
```

3. Inferential Statistics:

– **One-Sample T-Test**: Test if the mean math score is significantly different from 85.

```
t_stat, p_value =
stats.ttest_1samp(df['Math'], 85)
print(f"T-Statistic: {t_stat}, P-
Value: {p_value}")
```

– **Confidence Interval**: Calculate the 95% confidence interval for the mean science score.

```
conf_interval =
sm.stats.DescrStatsW(df['Science']).t
confint_mean()
print(f"95% Confidence Interval for
Science Score: {conf_interval}")
```

4. Correlation and Regression Analysis:

- **Correlation Coefficient**: Calculate the correlation between math and science scores.

  ```
  correlation =
  df['Math'].corr(df['Science'])
  print(f"Correlation between Math and
  Science: {correlation}")
  ```

- **Simple Linear Regression**: Model the relationship between math and science scores.

  ```
  X = sm.add_constant(df['Math'])
  Y = df['Science']
  model = sm.OLS(Y, X).fit()
  print(model.summary())
  ```

Example 2: Analyzing Time Series Data

1. **Loading the Data:**

   ```
   # Sample time series data
   data = {'Date':
   pd.date_range(start='2021-01-01',
   periods=12, freq='M'), 'Sales': [112,
   118, 132, 129, 121, 135, 148, 148,
   136, 119, 104, 118]}
   df = pd.DataFrame(data)
   ```

```
df.set_index('Date', inplace=True)
```

2. Time Series Decomposition:

```
decomposition =
sm.tsa.seasonal_decompose(df['Sales']
, model='additive')
decomposition.plot()
plt.show()
```

3. Moving Averages:

```
df['Rolling_Mean'] =
df['Sales'].rolling(window=3).mean()

plt.plot(df['Sales'],
label='Original')
plt.plot(df['Rolling_Mean'],
label='Rolling Mean')
plt.legend()
plt.show()
```

4. ARIMA Model:

```
model = ARIMA(df['Sales'], order=(1,
1, 1))
model_fit = model.fit()
```

```
print(model_fit.summary())

plt.plot(df['Sales'], 
label='Original')
plt.plot(model_fit.fittedvalues, 
label='Fitted')
plt.legend()
plt.show()
```

Conclusion

In this chapter, we explored a wide range of statistical analysis techniques using Python, including descriptive statistics, inferential statistics, hypothesis testing, correlation, regression analysis, time series analysis, and advanced statistical techniques. We demonstrated how to use libraries like NumPy, SciPy, Pandas, Statsmodels, and Scikit-learn to perform these analyses. By mastering these techniques, you will be well-equipped to analyse data, make informed decisions, and derive meaningful insights. As you continue to practice and apply these methods to real-world datasets, you'll find that Python provides a robust and flexible environment for statistical analysis.

Chapter 8: Introduction to Machine Learning

Introduction

Machine learning is a subset of artificial intelligence that enables systems to learn and improve from experience without being explicitly programmed. It involves training algorithms on data to make predictions or decisions. Python, with its rich ecosystem of libraries and frameworks, is a popular choice for implementing machine learning solutions. In this chapter, we will explore the basics of machine learning, including key concepts, types of machine learning, and practical examples using Python libraries such as Scikit-learn.

Key Concepts in Machine Learning

Before diving into the practical aspects, it's essential to understand some fundamental concepts in machine learning.

1. **Data and Features:**

   - **Data**: The raw information used to train machine learning models. It can be structured (e.g., CSV files, databases) or unstructured (e.g., images, text).

   - **Features**: The individual measurable properties or characteristics of the data. For example, in a dataset of houses, features might include the number of bedrooms, square footage, and location.

2. **Labels and Targets:**

- **Labels/Targets**: The outcome or value that the model is trying to predict. In supervised learning, each data point has a corresponding label.

3. **Training and Testing:**

    - **Training**: The process of feeding data to a machine learning algorithm to learn patterns and relationships.
    - **Testing**: The process of evaluating the model's performance on unseen data to assess its accuracy and generalisation.

4. **Overfitting and Underfitting:**

    - **Overfitting**: When a model learns the training data too well, capturing noise and outliers, leading to poor performance on new data.
    - **Underfitting**: When a model is too simple to capture the underlying patterns in the data, resulting in poor performance on both training and testing data.

Types of Machine Learning

Machine learning can be broadly categorised into three types: supervised learning, unsupervised learning, and reinforcement learning.

1. Supervised Learning:

In supervised learning, the model is trained on labeled data, meaning that each training example is paired with an output label. The goal is to learn a mapping from inputs to outputs that can be used to predict the labels of new, unseen data.

- **Classification**: The task of predicting a discrete label. For example, classifying emails as spam or not spam.
- **Regression**: The task of predicting a continuous value. For example, predicting house prices based on features like size and location.

2. Unsupervised Learning:

In unsupervised learning, the model is trained on unlabelled data, meaning that there are no output labels. The goal is to discover patterns, groupings, or structures in the data.

- **Clustering**: Grouping data points into clusters based on similarity. For example, customer segmentation in marketing.
- **Dimensionality Reduction**: Reducing the number of features while preserving the important information. For example, principal component analysis (PCA).

3. Reinforcement Learning:

In reinforcement learning, an agent learns to make decisions by interacting with an environment. The agent receives rewards or penalties based on its actions and learns to maximise cumulative rewards.

Machine Learning Workflow

A typical machine learning workflow involves several key steps:

1. **Data Collection**: Gathering the data needed for the problem.
2. **Data Preprocessing**: Cleaning and preparing the data for analysis.
3. **Feature Engineering**: Creating and selecting the most relevant features.
4. **Model Selection**: Choosing the appropriate machine learning algorithm.
5. **Model Training**: Training the model on the training data.
6. **Model Evaluation**: Evaluating the model's performance on the testing data.
7. **Hyperparameter Tuning**: Optimising the model's hyperparameters to improve performance.
8. **Model Deployment**: Deploying the model to a production environment for real-world use.

Practical Machine Learning with Scikit-learn

Scikit-learn is one of the most popular machine learning libraries in Python. It provides simple and efficient tools for data mining and data analysis. Let's explore some practical examples using Scikit-learn.

1. Installing Scikit-learn:

If you don't already have Scikit-learn installed, you can install it using pip:

```
pip install scikit-learn
```

2. Loading a Dataset:

Scikit-learn provides several built-in datasets that can be used for practice and experimentation. We'll use the Iris dataset for our examples.

```
from sklearn.datasets import load_iris

# Load the Iris dataset
iris = load_iris()
X, y = iris.data, iris.target
```

3. Data Preprocessing:

Data preprocessing involves cleaning and transforming the data to make it suitable for analysis. Common preprocessing steps include scaling, encoding categorical variables, and handling missing values.

- **Scaling**: Standardising the features by removing the mean and scaling to unit variance.

```
from sklearn.preprocessing import StandardScaler

# Standardize the features
scaler = StandardScaler()
X_scaled = scaler.fit_transform(X)
```

4. Splitting the Data:

Splitting the data into training and testing sets is essential for evaluating the model's performance.

```
from sklearn.model_selection import train_test_split

# Split the data into training and testing sets
X_train, X_test, y_train, y_test = train_test_split(X_scaled, y, test_size=0.3, random_state=42)
```

5. Model Selection and Training:

Scikit-learn provides a wide range of machine learning algorithms. We'll start with a simple classification algorithm: the k-nearest neighbours (KNN) classifier.

```
from sklearn.neighbors import KNeighborsClassifier

# Create a KNN classifier
knn = KNeighborsClassifier(n_neighbors=3)

# Train the model
knn.fit(X_train, y_train)
```

6. Model Evaluation:

Evaluating the model's performance is crucial to understand how well it generalises to new data. Common evaluation metrics for classification include accuracy, precision, recall, and F1-score.

```
from sklearn.metrics import
accuracy_score, classification_report

# Predict the labels of the test set
y_pred = knn.predict(X_test)

# Calculate accuracy
accuracy = accuracy_score(y_test,
y_pred)
print(f"Accuracy: {accuracy}")

# Print classification report
print(classification_report(y_test,
y_pred,
target_names=iris.target_names))
```

7. Hyperparameter Tuning:

Hyperparameter tuning involves optimising the algorithm's hyperparameters to improve performance. Grid search and random search are common techniques for hyperparameter tuning.

– **Grid Search**:

```
from sklearn.model_selection import
GridSearchCV

# Define the parameter grid
```

```
param_grid = {'n_neighbors': [1, 3,
5, 7, 9]}

# Create a grid search object
grid_search = GridSearchCV(knn,
param_grid, cv=5)

# Fit the grid search to the data
grid_search.fit(X_train, y_train)

# Print the best parameters and best
score
print(f"Best parameters:
{grid_search.best_params_}")
print(f"Best score:
{grid_search.best_score_}")
```

Supervised Learning: Classification

Classification is a supervised learning task that involves predicting a discrete label. Let's explore some popular classification algorithms.

1. Logistic Regression:

Logistic regression models the probability that a given input belongs to a particular class.

```
from sklearn.linear_model import
LogisticRegression

# Create a logistic regression
classifier
```

```
log_reg = LogisticRegression()

# Train the model
log_reg.fit(X_train, y_train)

# Evaluate the model
y_pred = log_reg.predict(X_test)
print(classification_report(y_test,
y_pred,
target_names=iris.target_names))
```

2. Decision Trees:

Decision trees partition the data into subsets based on the most significant features.

```
from sklearn.tree import
DecisionTreeClassifier

# Create a decision tree classifier
tree = DecisionTreeClassifier()

# Train the model
tree.fit(X_train, y_train)

# Evaluate the model
y_pred = tree.predict(X_test)
print(classification_report(y_test,
y_pred,
target_names=iris.target_names))
```

3. Random Forests:

Random forests are an ensemble method that combines multiple decision trees to improve performance.

```
from sklearn.ensemble import RandomForestClassifier

# Create a random forest classifier
forest = RandomForestClassifier(n_estimators=100)

# Train the model
forest.fit(X_train, y_train)

# Evaluate the model
y_pred = forest.predict(X_test)
print(classification_report(y_test, y_pred, target_names=iris.target_names))
```

Supervised Learning: Regression

Regression is a supervised learning task that involves predicting a continuous value. Let's explore some popular regression algorithms.

1. Linear Regression:

Linear regression models the relationship between the dependent variable and one or more independent variables.

```
from sklearn.linear_model import LinearRegression
```

```python
from sklearn.metrics import mean_squared_error

# Load the Boston housing dataset
from sklearn.datasets import load_boston
boston = load_boston()
X, y = boston.data, boston.target

# Standardize the features
scaler = StandardScaler()
X_scaled = scaler.fit_transform(X)

# Split the data into training and testing sets
X_train, X_test, y_train, y_test = train_test_split(X_scaled, y, test_size=0.3, random_state=42)

# Create a linear
 regression model
lin_reg = LinearRegression()

# Train the model
lin_reg.fit(X_train, y_train)

# Evaluate the model
y_pred = lin_reg.predict(X_test)
mse = mean_squared_error(y_test, y_pred)
```

```
print(f"Mean Squared Error: {mse}")
```

2. Ridge Regression:

Ridge regression is a regularised version of linear regression that includes a penalty term to prevent overfitting.

```
from sklearn.linear_model import Ridge

# Create a ridge regression model
ridge = Ridge(alpha=1.0)

# Train the model
ridge.fit(X_train, y_train)

# Evaluate the model
y_pred = ridge.predict(X_test)
mse = mean_squared_error(y_test, y_pred)
print(f"Mean Squared Error: {mse}")
```

3. Lasso Regression:

Lasso regression is another regularised version of linear regression that includes a penalty term, which can lead to sparse models.

```
from sklearn.linear_model import Lasso

# Create a lasso regression model
lasso = Lasso(alpha=0.1)
```

```
# Train the model
lasso.fit(X_train, y_train)

# Evaluate the model
y_pred = lasso.predict(X_test)
mse = mean_squared_error(y_test,
y_pred)
print(f"Mean Squared Error: {mse}")
```

Unsupervised Learning: Clustering

Clustering is an unsupervised learning task that involves grouping data points into clusters based on similarity. Let's explore some popular clustering algorithms.

1. K-Means Clustering:

K-means clustering partitions the data into k clusters, where each data point belongs to the cluster with the nearest mean.

```
from sklearn.cluster import KMeans

# Load the Iris dataset
X, y = iris.data, iris.target

# Standardize the features
scaler = StandardScaler()
X_scaled = scaler.fit_transform(X)

# Create a KMeans model
```

```
kmeans = KMeans(n_clusters=3,
random_state=42)

# Fit the model
kmeans.fit(X_scaled)

# Predict the cluster labels
cluster_labels =
kmeans.predict(X_scaled)

# Evaluate the model
print(f"Cluster Centers:
{kmeans.cluster_centers_}")
```

2. Hierarchical Clustering:

Hierarchical clustering builds a hierarchy of clusters by recursively merging or splitting clusters.

```
from scipy.cluster.hierarchy import
dendrogram, linkage

# Create a linkage matrix
Z = linkage(X_scaled, 'ward')

# Plot the dendrogram
plt.figure(figsize=(10, 7))
dendrogram(Z,
labels=iris.target_names[y])
plt.title('Dendrogram')
plt.xlabel('Samples')
plt.ylabel('Distance')
```

```
plt.show()
```

3. DBSCAN (Density-Based Spatial Clustering of Applications with Noise):

DBSCAN clusters data points based on density and can identify outliers.

```
from sklearn.cluster import DBSCAN

# Create a DBSCAN model
dbscan = DBSCAN(eps=0.5,
min_samples=5)

# Fit the model
dbscan.fit(X_scaled)

# Predict the cluster labels
cluster_labels = dbscan.labels_

# Evaluate the model
print(f"Cluster Labels:
{set(cluster_labels)}")
```

Dimensionality Reduction

Dimensionality reduction reduces the number of features while preserving the important information. Let's explore some popular dimensionality reduction techniques.

1. **Principal Component Analysis (PCA):**

PCA reduces the dimensionality of data by projecting it onto a lower-dimensional subspace.

```
from sklearn.decomposition import PCA

# Create a PCA model
pca = PCA(n_components=2)

# Fit the model
X_pca = pca.fit_transform(X_scaled)

# Plot the PCA-transformed data
plt.figure(figsize=(8, 6))
plt.scatter(X_pca[:, 0], X_pca[:, 1],
c=y, cmap='viridis')
plt.xlabel('Principal Component 1')
plt.ylabel('Principal Component 2')
plt.title('PCA of Iris Dataset')
plt.colorbar()
plt.show()
```

2. t-SNE (t-Distributed Stochastic Neighbour Embedding):

t-SNE is a technique for visualising high-dimensional data in a lower-dimensional space.

```
from sklearn.manifold import TSNE

# Create a t-SNE model
tsne = TSNE(n_components=2,
random_state=42)

# Fit the model
X_tsne = tsne.fit_transform(X_scaled)
```

```
# Plot the t-SNE-transformed data
plt.figure(figsize=(8, 6))
plt.scatter(X_tsne[:, 0], X_tsne[:,
1], c=y, cmap='viridis')
plt.xlabel('t-SNE Component 1')
plt.ylabel('t-SNE Component 2')
plt.title('t-SNE of Iris Dataset')
plt.colorbar()
plt.show()
```

Model Evaluation and Validation

Evaluating and validating machine learning models is crucial to ensure their performance and generalisation. Let's explore some common techniques.

1. Cross-Validation:

Cross-validation is a technique for assessing how a model generalises to new data by splitting the data into multiple training and testing sets.

```
from sklearn.model_selection import
cross_val_score

# Create a logistic regression model
log_reg = LogisticRegression()

# Perform cross-validation
cv_scores = cross_val_score(log_reg,
X_scaled, y, cv=5)
```

```
# Print the cross-validation scores
print(f"Cross-Validation Scores:
{cv_scores}")
print(f"Mean Cross-Validation Score:
{cv_scores.mean()}")
```

2. Confusion Matrix:

A confusion matrix summarises the performance of a classification model by showing the true positives, false positives, true negatives, and false negatives.

```
from sklearn.metrics import
confusion_matrix,
ConfusionMatrixDisplay

# Train the logistic regression model
log_reg.fit(X_train, y_train)

# Predict the labels of the test set
y_pred = log_reg.predict(X_test)

# Calculate the confusion matrix
conf_matrix =
confusion_matrix(y_test, y_pred)

# Plot the confusion matrix
disp =
ConfusionMatrixDisplay(confusion_matr
ix=conf_matrix,
display_labels=iris.target_names)
disp.plot()
```

```
plt.show()
```

3. ROC Curve and AUC:

The ROC curve plots the true positive rate against the false positive rate at various threshold settings, and the AUC (Area Under the Curve) measures the overall performance of the model.

```
from sklearn.metrics import
roc_curve, roc_auc_score

# Calculate the predicted
probabilities
y_proba =
log_reg.predict_proba(X_test)[:, 1]

# Calculate the ROC curve
fpr, tpr, thresholds =
roc_curve(y_test, y_proba,
pos_label=1)

# Plot the ROC curve
plt.figure(figsize=(8, 6))
plt.plot(fpr, tpr, marker='.')
plt.xlabel('False Positive Rate')
plt.ylabel('True Positive Rate')
plt.title('ROC Curve')
plt.show()

# Calculate the AUC
auc = roc_auc_score(y_test, y_proba)
```

```
print(f"AUC: {auc}")
```

Practical Examples

To solidify your understanding of machine learning with Python, let's walk through practical examples using sample datasets.

Example 1: Predicting Breast Cancer

1. **Loading the Data:**

```
from sklearn.datasets import load_breast_cancer

# Load the Breast Cancer dataset
cancer = load_breast_cancer()
X, y = cancer.data, cancer.target
```

2. **Data Preprocessing:**

```
# Standardize the features
scaler = StandardScaler()
X_scaled = scaler.fit_transform(X)
```

3. **Splitting the Data:**

```
# Split the data into training and
testing sets
X_train, X_test, y_train, y_test =
train_test_split(X_scaled, y,
test_size=0.3, random_state=42)
```

4. **Model Selection and Training:**

– **Logistic Regression:**

```
log_reg = LogisticRegression()
log_reg.fit(X_train, y_train)
```

5. **Model Evaluation:**

```
y_pred = log_reg.predict(X_test)
print(classification_report(y_test,
y_pred,
target_names=cancer.target_names))
```

Example 2: Clustering Wine Types

1. **Loading the Data:**

```
from sklearn.datasets import
load_wine
```

```
# Load the Wine dataset
wine = load_wine()
X, y = wine.data, wine.target
```

2. **Data Preprocessing:**

```
# Standardize the features
scaler = StandardScaler()
X_scaled = scaler.fit_transform(X)
```

3. **K-Means Clustering:**

```
kmeans = KMeans(n_clusters=3,
random_state=42)
kmeans.fit(X_scaled)
cluster_labels =
kmeans.predict(X_scaled)
```

4. **PCA for Visualization:**

```
pca = PCA(n_components=2)
X_pca = pca.fit_transform(X_scaled)

plt.figure(figsize=(8, 6))
plt.scatter(X_pca[:, 0], X_pca[:, 1],
c=cluster_labels, cmap='viridis')
plt.xlabel('Principal Component 1')
```

```
plt.ylabel('Principal Component 2')
plt.title('PCA of Wine Dataset')
plt.colorbar()
plt.show()
```

Conclusion

In this chapter, we explored the basics of machine learning, including key concepts, types of machine learning, and a typical machine learning workflow. We demonstrated how to implement various machine learning algorithms using Python's Scikit-learn library, covering classification, regression, clustering, dimensionality reduction, and model evaluation. By mastering these techniques, you'll be well-equipped
 to build and deploy machine learning models to solve real-world problems. As you continue to practice and apply these methods to diverse datasets, you'll find that Python provides a robust and flexible environment for machine learning.

Chapter 9: Working with Text Data

Introduction

Text data is ubiquitous in the modern world, from social media posts and emails to research papers and books. Analysing and processing text data can provide valuable insights and enable a wide range of applications, including sentiment analysis, language translation, and information retrieval. Python, with its rich ecosystem of libraries, offers powerful tools for working with text data. In this chapter, we will explore techniques for handling, processing, and analysing text data using libraries such as NLTK (Natural Language Toolkit) and spaCy.

Basics of Text Data

Before diving into the tools and techniques, it's essential to understand the basic concepts of text data processing.

1. **Tokens and Tokenisation:**

   - **Tokens**: Tokens are the individual pieces of text, such as words or punctuation marks.

   - **Tokenisation**: The process of splitting text into tokens. Tokenisation is a crucial first step in text processing.

2. **Text Normalisation:**

   Text normalisation involves transforming text into a standard format, which can include:

- **Lowercasing**: Converting all characters to lowercase to ensure uniformity.

- **Removing Punctuation**: Eliminating punctuation marks to focus on the words.

- **Stemming**: Reducing words to their base or root form (e.g., "running" to "run").

- **Lemmatisation**: Converting words to their base form using vocabulary and morphological analysis (e.g., "better" to "good").

3. **Stop Words:**

Stop words are common words (e.g., "and," "the," "is") that are often removed from text data as they provide little meaningful information.

Working with NLTK

The Natural Language Toolkit (NLTK) is one of the most popular libraries for working with text data in Python. It provides tools for tokenisation, stemming, lemmatisation, and more.

1. **Installing NLTK:**

If you don't already have NLTK installed, you can install it using pip:

```
pip install nltk
```

2. **Tokenisation:**

NLTK provides functions for tokenising text into sentences and words.

```
import nltk
nltk.download('punkt')
from nltk.tokenize import
sent_tokenize, word_tokenize

text = "Hello world. This is a test."

# Sentence tokenization
sentences = sent_tokenize(text)
print(sentences)

# Word tokenization
words = word_tokenize(text)
print(words)
```

3. Text Normalisation:

– **Lowercasing and Removing Punctuation**:

```
import string

text = "Hello, World!"
text = text.lower()
text =
text.translate(str.maketrans('', '',
string.punctuation))
print(text)
```

– **Stemming**:

```
from nltk.stem import PorterStemmer

stemmer = PorterStemmer()
words = ["running", "jumps",
"easily", "fairly"]
stemmed_words = [stemmer.stem(word)
for word in words]
print(stemmed_words)
```

– **Lemmatisation**:

```
from nltk.stem import
WordNetLemmatizer
nltk.download('wordnet')

lemmatizer = WordNetLemmatizer()
words = ["running", "jumps",
"easily", "fairly"]
lemmatized_words =
[lemmatizer.lemmatize(word) for word
in words]
print(lemmatized_words)
```

4. Removing Stop Words:

```
from nltk.corpus import stopwords
nltk.download('stopwords')

stop_words =
set(stopwords.words('english'))
```

```
words = ["This", "is", "a", "simple",
"test"]
filtered_words = [word for word in
words if word.lower() not in
stop_words]
print(filtered_words)
```

Advanced Text Processing with spaCy

spaCy is another powerful library for advanced text processing and natural language understanding. It is designed for production use and provides features such as tokenisation, part-of-speech tagging, named entity recognition, and more.

1. Installing spaCy:

If you don't already have spaCy installed, you can install it using pip:

```
pip install spacy
python -m spacy download
en_core_web_sm
```

2. Tokenisation and Text Normalisation:

spaCy provides an easy-to-use API for tokenisation and text normalisation.

```
import spacy

nlp = spacy.load("en_core_web_sm")
text = "Hello, World! This is a
test."
```

143

```
# Process the text
doc = nlp(text)

# Tokenization
tokens = [token.text for token in
doc]
print(tokens)

# Text normalization
normalized_tokens = [token.lemma_ for
token in doc if not token.is_stop and
not token.is_punct]
print(normalized_tokens)
```

3. Part-of-Speech Tagging:

Part-of-speech tagging assigns a part of speech (e.g., noun, verb, adjective) to each token.

```
# Process the text
doc = nlp("The quick brown fox jumps
over the lazy dog.")

# Part-of-speech tagging
pos_tags = [(token.text, token.pos_)
for token in doc]
print(pos_tags)
```

4. Named Entity Recognition:

Named entity recognition identifies and classifies named entities (e.g., people, organisations, locations) in text.

```
# Process the text
doc = nlp("Apple is looking at buying
U.K. startup for $1 billion.")

# Named entity recognition
entities = [(entity.text,
entity.label_) for entity in
doc.ents]
print(entities)
```

5. Dependency Parsing:

Dependency parsing analyses the grammatical structure of a sentence and establishes relationships between "head" words and words that modify those heads.

```
# Process the text
doc = nlp("The quick brown fox jumps
over the lazy dog.")

# Dependency parsing
for token in doc:
    print(f"{token.text}
({token.dep_}): {token.head.text}")
```

Text Classification

Text classification is the task of assigning predefined categories to text. It is widely used in applications such as spam detection, sentiment analysis, and topic categorisation.

1. Preparing the Data:

For text classification, you typically need labeled data. We'll use the 20 Newsgroups dataset for our example.

```
from sklearn.datasets import
fetch_20newsgroups

# Load the dataset
categories = ['alt.atheism',
'soc.religion.christian',
'comp.graphics', 'sci.med']
newsgroups =
fetch_20newsgroups(subset='train',
categories=categories)

# Display some information about the
dataset
print(newsgroups.target_names)
print(len(newsgroups.data))
print(newsgroups.data[0])
```

2. Text Vectorization:

Text data needs to be converted into numerical format for machine learning algorithms to process it. The `CountVectorizer` and `TfidfVectorizer` from Scikit-learn are commonly used for this purpose.

– **Count Vectorisation**:

```
from sklearn.feature_extraction.text
import CountVectorizer
```

```python
# Create a CountVectorizer
count_vect = CountVectorizer()
X_train_counts =
count_vect.fit_transform(newsgroups.d
ata)
print(X_train_counts.shape)
```

– **TF-IDF Vectorisation**:

```python
from sklearn.feature_extraction.text
import TfidfVectorizer

# Create a TfidfVectorizer
tfidf_vect = TfidfVectorizer()
X_train_tfidf =
tfidf_vect.fit_transform(newsgroups.d
ata)
print(X_train_tfidf.shape)
```

3. Building a Text Classification Model:
We'll use a Naive Bayes classifier for this example.

```python
from sklearn.naive_bayes import
MultinomialNB
from sklearn.pipeline import Pipeline

# Create a pipeline
text_clf = Pipeline([
    ('tfidf', TfidfVectorizer()),
    ('clf', MultinomialNB())
```

```
])

# Train the model
text_clf.fit(newsgroups.data,
newsgroups.target)
```

4. Evaluating the Model:

We'll evaluate the model using the test subset of the 20 Newsgroups dataset.

```
# Load the test dataset
newsgroups_test =
fetch_20newsgroups(subset='test',
categories=categories)

# Predict the labels of the test set
predicted =
text_clf.predict(newsgroups_test.data
)

# Calculate accuracy
from sklearn import metrics
accuracy =
metrics.accuracy_score(newsgroups_tes
t.target, predicted)
print(f"Accuracy: {accuracy}")

# Print a classification report
print(metrics.classification_report(n
ewsgroups_test.target, predicted,
```

```
target_names=newsgroups.target_names)
)
```

Sentiment Analysis

Sentiment analysis is the task of determining the sentiment or emotion expressed in a piece of text. It is widely used in applications such as social media monitoring and customer feedback analysis.

1. Using NLTK's VADER Sentiment Analyzer:

VADER (Valence Aware Dictionary and Sentiment Reasoner) is a lexicon and rule-based sentiment analysis tool.

```
from nltk.sentiment.vader import SentimentIntensityAnalyzer
nltk.download('vader_lexicon')

# Create a SentimentIntensityAnalyzer
sia = SentimentIntensityAnalyzer()

# Analyze the sentiment of a sentence


text = "I love this product! It's amazing."
sentiment = sia.polarity_scores(text)
print(sentiment)
```

2. Using TextBlob:

TextBlob is a simple library for processing textual data. It provides a straightforward API for common natural language processing (NLP) tasks, including sentiment analysis.

```
from textblob import TextBlob

# Analyze the sentiment of a sentence
text = "I love this product! It's amazing."
blob = TextBlob(text)
print(blob.sentiment)
```

Topic Modeling

Topic modelling is the task of identifying topics that best describe a set of documents. Latent Dirichlet Allocation (LDA) is a popular topic modelling technique.

1. Preparing the Data:
We'll use the 20 Newsgroups dataset for topic modelling.

```
from sklearn.feature_extraction.text import CountVectorizer

# Load the dataset
newsgroups = fetch_20newsgroups(subset='all', categories=categories)

# Vectorize the text data
count_vect = CountVectorizer(stop_words='english')
```

```
X_counts = 
count_vect.fit_transform(newsgroups.d
ata)
```

2. Building an LDA Model:

We'll use Scikit-learn's `LatentDirichletAllocation` for topic modelling.

```
from sklearn.decomposition import
LatentDirichletAllocation

# Create an LDA model
lda =
LatentDirichletAllocation(n_component
s=5, random_state=42)

# Fit the model
lda.fit(X_counts)

# Display the topics
for index, topic in
enumerate(lda.components_):
    print(f"Topic {index + 1}")

print([count_vect.get_feature_names()
[i] for i in topic.argsort()[-10:]])
```

Named Entity Recognition (NER)

Named Entity Recognition (NER) is the task of identifying and classifying named entities (e.g., people, organisations, locations) in text. We'll use spaCy for NER.

1. Using spaCy for NER:

```
import spacy

# Load the spaCy model
nlp = spacy.load("en_core_web_sm")

# Process the text
text = "Apple is looking at buying U.K. startup for $1 billion."
doc = nlp(text)

# Display the named entities
for entity in doc.ents:
    print(f"{entity.text} ({entity.label_})")
```

Working with Large Text Corpora

When working with large text corpora, it is essential to efficiently manage and process the data. NLTK provides tools for handling large corpora.

1. Loading a Large Corpus:

We'll use the Gutenberg corpus from NLTK for this example.

```
import nltk
nltk.download('gutenberg')

from nltk.corpus import gutenberg

# Display the file IDs in the
Gutenberg corpus
print(gutenberg.fileids())

# Load a specific text
text = gutenberg.raw('austen-
emma.txt')
print(text[:500])
```

2. Processing the Corpus:

You can apply various text processing techniques to the entire corpus.

```
from nltk.tokenize import
word_tokenize
from nltk.probability import FreqDist

# Tokenize the text
tokens = word_tokenize(text)

# Calculate the frequency
distribution of words
freq_dist = FreqDist(tokens)

# Display the most common words
```

```
print(freq_dist.most_common(10))
```

Practical Example: Analysing Customer Reviews

To solidify your understanding of working with text data, let's walk through a practical example of analysing customer reviews.

1. **Loading the Data:**

We'll use a dataset of Amazon product reviews for this example.

```
import pandas as pd

# Load the dataset
df = pd.read_csv('amazon_reviews.csv')

# Display the first few rows
print(df.head())
```

2. **Data Preprocessing:**

We'll preprocess the text data by tokenising, normalising, and removing stop words.

```
import nltk
from nltk.corpus import stopwords
from nltk.tokenize import word_tokenize
```

```python
import string

nltk.download('punkt')
nltk.download('stopwords')

# Define a function for text preprocessing
def preprocess_text(text):
    # Tokenize the text
    tokens = word_tokenize(text)
    # Lowercase the tokens
    tokens = [token.lower() for token in tokens]
    # Remove punctuation
    tokens = [token for token in tokens if token.isalpha()]
    # Remove stop words
    stop_words = set(stopwords.words('english'))
    tokens = [token for token in tokens if token not in stop_words]
    return ' '.join(tokens)

# Apply the preprocessing function to the review text
df['processed_review'] = df['reviewText'].apply(preprocess_text)
print(df['processed_review'].head())
```

3. Sentiment Analysis:

We'll use TextBlob to analyse the sentiment of the reviews.

```
from textblob import TextBlob

# Define a function to analyze
sentiment
def analyze_sentiment(text):
    blob = TextBlob(text)
    return blob.sentiment.polarity

# Apply the sentiment analysis
function to the processed reviews
df['sentiment'] =
df['processed_review'].apply(analyze_
sentiment)
print(df[['reviewText',
'sentiment']].head())
```

4. Visualising the Results:

We'll create visualisations to understand the distribution of sentiments.

```
import matplotlib.pyplot as plt
import seaborn as sns

# Plot the distribution of sentiment
scores
plt.figure(figsize=(10, 6))
```

```
sns.histplot(df['sentiment'],
bins=30, kde=True)
plt.xlabel('Sentiment Score')
plt.ylabel('Frequency')
plt.title('Distribution of Sentiment
Scores')
plt.show()
```

5. **Topic Modeling:**

We'll use LDA to identify topics in the customer reviews.

```
from sklearn.feature_extraction.text
import CountVectorizer
from sklearn.decomposition import
LatentDirichletAllocation

# Vectorize the processed reviews
count_vect =
CountVectorizer(stop_words='english')
X_counts =
count_vect.fit_transform(df['processe
d_review'])

# Create an LDA model
lda =
LatentDirichletAllocation(n_component
s=5, random_state=42)

# Fit the model
```

```
lda.fit(X_counts)

# Display the topics
for index, topic in
enumerate(lda.components_):
    print(f"Topic {index + 1}")

print([count_vect.get_feature_names()
[i] for i in topic.argsort()[-10:]])
```

Conclusion

In this chapter, we explored various techniques for working with text data using Python. We covered the basics of text data processing, including tokenisation, text normalisation, and removing stop words. We demonstrated how to use NLTK and spaCy for advanced text processing tasks such as part-of-speech tagging, named entity recognition, and dependency parsing. We also explored text classification, sentiment analysis, topic modelling, and named entity recognition. By mastering these techniques, you'll be well-equipped to analyse and process text data for a wide range of applications. As you continue to practice and apply these methods to real-world datasets, you'll find that Python provides a robust and flexible environment for working with text data.

Chapter 10: Time Series Analysis

Introduction

Time series analysis involves analysing and modelling data points collected or recorded at specific time intervals. Time series data is ubiquitous, appearing in various fields such as finance, economics, weather forecasting, and many others. Understanding time series data and how to analyse it is essential for making informed decisions based on historical trends and patterns. In this chapter, we will explore the fundamentals of time series analysis using Python, covering topics such as time series decomposition, forecasting, and advanced techniques like ARIMA and seasonal decomposition.

Basics of Time Series Data

Before diving into the analysis techniques, it is essential to understand the basic concepts of time series data.

1. Time Series Data:

Time series data is a sequence of data points recorded at successive points in time, typically with equal intervals between them. Examples include daily stock prices, monthly sales figures, and annual GDP growth rates.

2. Components of a Time Series:

A time series can be decomposed into several components:

- **Trend**: The long-term movement or direction in the data.

- **Seasonality**: Regular patterns or cycles in the data that occur at fixed intervals (e.g., monthly, quarterly).

- **Cyclical**: Long-term fluctuations in the data that are not of a fixed frequency.

- **Irregular/Residual**: Random noise or anomalies in the data that cannot be attributed to trend, seasonality, or cyclical components.

Working with Time Series Data in Python

Python provides powerful libraries for handling and analysing time series data, including Pandas, Statsmodels, and Scikit-learn.

1. Loading and Exploring Time Series Data:

We'll start by loading and exploring a sample time series dataset using Pandas.

```
import pandas as pd

# Load the dataset
df = pd.read_csv('time_series_data.csv',
parse_dates=['Date'],
index_col='Date')

# Display the first few rows
print(df.head())
```

```
# Display basic information about the
dataset
print(df.info())

# Plot the time series data
df.plot(figsize=(10, 6))
plt.xlabel('Date')
plt.ylabel('Value')
plt.title('Time Series Data')
plt.show()
```

2. Handling Missing Data:

Time series data often contains missing values. Proper handling of missing data is crucial for accurate analysis and modelling.

```
# Check for missing values
print(df.isnull().sum())

# Fill missing values using forward
fill
df_filled = df.fillna(method='ffill')

# Display the filled dataset
print(df_filled.head())
```

Time Series Decomposition

Time series decomposition involves breaking down a time series into its components: trend, seasonality, and residuals.

This helps in understanding the underlying patterns and structures in the data.

1. Decomposition using Statsmodels:

Statsmodels provides tools for additive and multiplicative decomposition of time series data.

```
import statsmodels.api as sm

# Decompose the time series
decomposition = sm.tsa.seasonal_decompose(df['Value']
, model='additive')

# Plot the decomposed components
decomposition.plot()
plt.show()
```

2. Additive and Multiplicative Decomposition:

- **Additive Decomposition**: Used when the components of the time series (trend, seasonality, and residuals) are added together.

- **Multiplicative Decomposition**: Used when the components are multiplied together.

Example:

```
# Additive decomposition
decomposition_add = sm.tsa.seasonal_decompose(df['Value']
, model='additive')
```

```
decomposition_add.plot()
plt.show()

# Multiplicative decomposition
decomposition_mult =
sm.tsa.seasonal_decompose(df['Value']
, model='multiplicative')
decomposition_mult.plot()
plt.show()
```

Time Series Forecasting

Forecasting involves predicting future values of a time series based on its historical patterns. There are various methods for time series forecasting, including moving averages, exponential smoothing, and ARIMA models.

1. Moving Averages:

Moving averages smooth out short-term fluctuations and highlight longer-term trends.

```
# Calculate the rolling mean (moving average)
df['Rolling_Mean'] =
df['Value'].rolling(window=12).mean()

# Plot the original data and the rolling mean
plt.figure(figsize=(10, 6))
plt.plot(df['Value'],
label='Original')
```

```
plt.plot(df['Rolling_Mean'],
label='Rolling Mean', color='red')
plt.xlabel('Date')
plt.ylabel('Value')
plt.title('Moving Average')
plt.legend()
plt.show()
```

2. Exponential Smoothing:

Exponential smoothing assigns exponentially decreasing weights to past observations.

```
from statsmodels.tsa.holtwinters
import SimpleExpSmoothing

# Apply simple exponential smoothing
model =
SimpleExpSmoothing(df['Value'])
fitted_model =
model.fit(smoothing_level=0.2,
optimized=False)
df['SES'] = fitted_model.fittedvalues

# Plot the original data and the
smoothed values
plt.figure(figsize=(10, 6))
plt.plot(df['Value'],
label='Original')
plt.plot(df['SES'], label='SES',
color='red')
plt.xlabel('Date')
```

```
plt.ylabel('Value')
plt.title('Simple Exponential 
Smoothing')
plt.legend()
plt.show()
```

3. Holt-Winters Method:

The Holt-Winters method extends exponential smoothing to capture trend and seasonality.

```
from statsmodels.tsa.holtwinters 
import ExponentialSmoothing

# Apply Holt-Winters method
model = 
ExponentialSmoothing(df['Value'], 
trend='add', seasonal='add', 
seasonal_periods=12)
fitted_model = model.fit()
df['Holt_Winters'] = 
fitted_model.fittedvalues

# Plot the original data and the 
Holt-Winters fitted values
plt.figure(figsize=(10, 6))
plt.plot(df['Value'], 
label='Original')
plt.plot(df['Holt_Winters'], 
label='Holt-Winters', color='red')
plt.xlabel('Date')
plt.ylabel('Value')
```

```
plt.title('Holt-Winters Method')
plt.legend()
plt.show()
```

ARIMA Models

ARIMA (AutoRegressive Integrated Moving Average) models are widely used for time series forecasting. They combine autoregressive (AR) and moving average (MA) models with differencing to make the time series stationary.

1. Identifying the Parameters:

Before fitting an ARIMA model, you need to identify the order of the AR, I, and MA components. This involves determining the values of p (autoregressive order), d (differencing order), and q (moving average order).

2. Differencing:

Differencing is used to make the time series stationary.

```
# Calculate the difference
df['Diff'] = df['Value'].diff()

# Plot the differenced series
plt.figure(figsize=(10, 6))
plt.plot(df['Diff'].dropna(),
label='Differenced')
plt.xlabel('Date')
plt.ylabel('Value')
plt.title('Differenced Time Series')
plt.legend()
plt.show()
```

3. Autocorrelation and Partial Autocorrelation:

The autocorrelation function (ACF) and partial autocorrelation function (PACF) help in identifying the values of p and q.

```
from statsmodels.graphics.tsaplots
import plot_acf, plot_pacf

# Plot the ACF and PACF
plt.figure(figsize=(12, 6))
plt.subplot(121)
plot_acf(df['Value'].dropna(),
ax=plt.gca())
plt.subplot(122)
plot_pacf(df['Value'].dropna(),
ax=plt.gca())
plt.show()
```

4. Fitting an ARIMA Model:

Once the parameters are identified, you can fit the ARIMA model.

```
from statsmodels.tsa.arima.model
import ARIMA

# Fit the ARIMA model
model = ARIMA(df['Value'], order=(1,
1, 1))
fitted_model = model.fit()

# Print the model summary
```

```python
print(fitted_model.summary())

# Plot the original data and the fitted values
plt.figure(figsize=(10, 6))
plt.plot(df['Value'], label='Original')
plt.plot(fitted_model.fittedvalues, label='Fitted', color='red')
plt.xlabel('Date')
plt.ylabel('Value')
plt.title('ARIMA Model')
plt.legend()
plt.show()
```

5. **Forecasting with ARIMA:**
Use the fitted ARIMA model to forecast future values.

```python
# Forecast future values
forecast_steps = 12
forecast = fitted_model.forecast(steps=forecast_steps)
forecast_index = pd.date_range(start=df.index[-1], periods=forecast_steps + 1, closed='right')
forecast_series = pd.Series(forecast, index=forecast_index)
```

```
# Plot the original data and the
forecast
plt.figure(figsize=(10, 6))
plt.plot(df['Value'],
label='Original')
plt.plot(forecast_series,
label='Forecast', color='red')
plt.xlabel('Date')
plt.ylabel('Value')
plt.title('ARIMA Forecast')
plt.legend()
plt.show()
```

Seasonal Decomposition of Time Series (STL)

Seasonal-Trend decomposition using LOESS (STL) is a versatile method for decomposing time series data, particularly useful for series with seasonal components.

1. Applying STL Decomposition:

STL uses locally estimated scatterplot smoothing (LOESS) to extract the components of the time series.

```
from statsmodels.tsa.seasonal import STL

# Apply STL decomposition

stl = STL(df['Value'], seasonal=13)
result = stl.fit()
```

```python
# Plot the STL components
fig = result.plot()
plt.show()
```

Advanced Techniques in Time Series Analysis

Beyond the basic methods, there are advanced techniques for time series analysis that can handle more complex patterns and structures.

1. State Space Models:

State space models provide a flexible framework for modelling time series data with multiple components, including trend, seasonality, and irregular variations.

```
import statsmodels.api as sm

# Fit a state space model
model = sm.tsa.UnobservedComponents(df['Value'], level='local level', seasonal=12)
fitted_model = model.fit()

# Print the model summary
print(fitted_model.summary())

# Plot the original data and the fitted values
plt.figure(figsize=(10, 6))
plt.plot(df['Value'], label='Original')
```

```python
plt.plot(fitted_model.fittedvalues,
label='Fitted', color='red')
plt.xlabel('Date')
plt.ylabel('Value')
plt.title('State Space Model')
plt.legend()
plt.show()
```

2. Prophet:

Prophet is a forecasting tool developed by Facebook for time series data that exhibits strong seasonal effects and multiple seasonality.

```
from fbprophet import Prophet

# Prepare the data for Prophet
df_prophet =
df.reset_index().rename(columns={'Date': 'ds', 'Value': 'y'})

# Create a Prophet model
model = Prophet()
model.fit(df_prophet)

# Make a future dataframe for forecasting
future =
model.make_future_dataframe(periods=12, freq='M')

# Forecast the future values
```

```
forecast = model.predict(future)

# Plot the forecast
fig = model.plot(forecast)
plt.show()
```

3. GARCH (Generalised Autoregressive Conditional Heteroskedasticity):

GARCH models are used to model time series data with volatility clustering, common in financial time series.

```
from arch import arch_model

# Fit a GARCH model
model = arch_model(df['Value'],
vol='Garch', p=1, q=1)
fitted_model = model.fit()

# Print the model summary
print(fitted_model.summary())

# Plot the original data and the
fitted values
plt.figure(figsize=(10, 6))
plt.plot(df['Value'],
label='Original')
plt.plot(fitted_model.conditional_vol
atility, label='Fitted Volatility',
color='red')
plt.xlabel('Date')
plt.ylabel('Value')
```

```
plt.title('GARCH Model')
plt.legend()
plt.show()
```

Practical Example: Forecasting Monthly Sales

To solidify your understanding of time series analysis, let's walk through a practical example of forecasting monthly sales.

1. **Loading the Data:**

We'll use a dataset of monthly sales figures for this example.

```
import pandas as pd

# Load the dataset
df = pd.read_csv('monthly_sales.csv',
parse_dates=['Date'],
index_col='Date')

# Display the first few rows
print(df.head())

# Plot the time series data
df.plot(figsize=(10, 6))
plt.xlabel('Date')
plt.ylabel('Sales')
plt.title('Monthly Sales')
plt.show()
```

2. **Decomposition:**

Decompose the time series to understand its components.

```
import statsmodels.api as sm

# Decompose the time series
decomposition = sm.tsa.seasonal_decompose(df['Sales']
, model='multiplicative')

# Plot the decomposed components
decomposition.plot()
plt.show()
```

3. **ARIMA Model:**

Identify the parameters and fit an ARIMA model.

```
from statsmodels.tsa.arima.model import ARIMA

# Fit the ARIMA model
model = ARIMA(df['Sales'], order=(1, 1, 1))
fitted_model = model.fit()

# Print the model summary
print(fitted_model.summary())
```

```python
# Plot the original data and the
fitted values
plt.figure(figsize=(10, 6))
plt.plot(df['Sales'],
label='Original')
plt.plot(fitted_model.fittedvalues,
label='Fitted', color='red')
plt.xlabel('Date')
plt.ylabel('Sales')
plt.title('ARIMA Model')
plt.legend()
plt.show()
```

4. **Forecasting:**

Use the fitted ARIMA model to forecast future sales.

```python
# Forecast future sales
forecast_steps = 12
forecast =
fitted_model.forecast(steps=forecast_
steps)
forecast_index =
pd.date_range(start=df.index[-1],
periods=forecast_steps + 1,
closed='right')
forecast_series = pd.Series(forecast,
index=forecast_index)
```

```
# Plot the original data and the
forecast
plt.figure(figsize=(10, 6))
plt.plot(df['Sales'],
label='Original')
plt.plot(forecast_series,
label='Forecast', color='red')
plt.xlabel('Date')
plt.ylabel('Sales')
plt.title('Sales Forecast')
plt.legend()
plt.show()
```

5. **Prophet Model:**

Use Prophet to forecast future sales.

```
from fbprophet import Prophet

# Prepare the data for Prophet
df_prophet =
df.reset_index().rename(columns={'Dat
e': 'ds', 'Sales': 'y'})

# Create a Prophet model
model = Prophet()
model.fit(df_prophet)

# Make a future dataframe for
forecasting
```

```
future = 
model.make_future_dataframe(periods=1
2, freq='M')

# Forecast the future values
forecast = model.predict(future)

# Plot the forecast
fig = model.plot(forecast)
plt.show()
```

Conclusion

In this chapter, we explored the fundamentals of time series analysis using Python. We covered the basic concepts of time series data, including its components and how to handle missing values. We delved into time series decomposition, forecasting methods such as moving averages, exponential smoothing, and ARIMA models. We also explored advanced techniques like STL decomposition, state space models, and GARCH models. By mastering these techniques, you'll be well-equipped to analsze and forecast time series data for a wide range of applications. As you continue to practice and apply these methods to real-world datasets, you'll find that Python provides a robust and flexible environment for time series analysis.

Chapter 11: Advanced Topics

Introduction

As you advance in your Python journey, you'll encounter more complex and sophisticated concepts that can significantly enhance your programming skills and capabilities. This chapter covers advanced topics in Python, including object-oriented programming (OOP), decorators, context managers, metaclasses, concurrency, and parallelism. Mastering these topics will enable you to write more efficient, scalable, and maintainable code.

Object-Oriented Programming (OOP)

Object-oriented programming (OOP) is a programming paradigm based on the concept of "objects," which can contain data and code to manipulate that data. Python supports OOP and provides various features to implement it effectively.

1. Classes and Objects:

A class is a blueprint for creating objects. Objects are instances of classes.

```
class Dog:
    # Class attribute
    species = 'Canis familiaris'

    def __init__(self, name, age):
```

```python
        # Instance attributes
        self.name = name
        self.age = age

    # Instance method
    def bark(self):
        return f"{self.name} says woof!"

# Create an instance of the Dog class
my_dog = Dog("Buddy", 3)

# Access attributes and methods
print(my_dog.name)    # Outputs: Buddy
print(my_dog.age)     # Outputs: 3
print(my_dog.bark())  # Outputs: Buddy says woof!
```

2. Inheritance:

Inheritance allows a class to inherit attributes and methods from another class.

```python
class Animal:
    def __init__(self, name):
        self.name = name

    def speak(self):
        raise NotImplementedError("Subclass must implement abstract method")
```

```
class Dog(Animal):
    def speak(self):
        return f"{self.name} says woof!"

class Cat(Animal):
    def speak(self):
        return f"{self.name} says meow!"

# Create instances of Dog and Cat
dog = Dog("Buddy")
cat = Cat("Whiskers")

print(dog.speak())  # Outputs: Buddy says woof!
print(cat.speak())  # Outputs: Whiskers says meow!
```

3. Encapsulation:

Encapsulation restricts access to certain methods and variables to prevent accidental modification of data.

```
class Car:
    def __init__(self, make, model):
        self._make = make    # Protected attribute
        self.__model = model  # Private attribute

    def get_make(self):
```

```
        return self._make

    def set_make(self, make):
        self._make = make

    def get_model(self):
        return self.__model

    def set_model(self, model):
        self.__model = model

# Create an instance of the Car class
my_car = Car("Toyota", "Corolla")

print(my_car.get_make())   # Outputs: Toyota
print(my_car.get_model())  # Outputs: Corolla
```

4. Polymorphism:

Polymorphism allows methods to be used interchangeably between different classes that implement the same interface.

```
class Bird:
    def speak(self):
        return "Chirp!"

class Duck(Bird):
    def speak(self):
        return "Quack!"
```

```
class Parrot(Bird):
    def speak(self):
        return "Squawk!"

def make_bird_speak(bird):
    print(bird.speak())

duck = Duck()
parrot = Parrot()

make_bird_speak(duck)      # Outputs: Quack!
make_bird_speak(parrot)    # Outputs: Squawk!
```

Decorators

Decorators are a powerful feature in Python that allows you to modify the behaviour of functions or classes. They are used to wrap another function or method to extend its behaviour without explicitly modifying it.

1. Function Decorators:

A function decorator is a higher-order function that takes a function as an argument and returns a new function with extended behaviour.

```
def my_decorator(func):
    def wrapper():
        print("Something is happening before the function is called.")
        func()
```

```
        print("Something is happening
after the function is called.")
    return wrapper

@my_decorator
def say_hello():
    print("Hello!")

say_hello()
# Outputs:
# Something is happening before the
function is called.
# Hello!
# Something is happening after the
function is called.
```

2. Class Decorators:

Class decorators are used to modify the behaviour of classes.

```
def singleton(cls):
    instances = {}
    def get_instance(*args,
**kwargs):
        if cls not in instances:
            instances[cls] =
cls(*args, **kwargs)
        return instances[cls]
    return get_instance

@singleton
```

```
class MyClass:
    pass

a = MyClass()
b = MyClass()

print(a is b)   # Outputs: True
```

3. Parameterised Decorators:
Parameterised decorators allow you to pass arguments to the decorator.

```
def repeat(n):
    def decorator(func):
        def wrapper(*args, **kwargs):
            for _ in range(n):
                func(*args, **kwargs)
        return wrapper
    return decorator

@repeat(3)
def say_hello():
    print("Hello!")

say_hello()
# Outputs:
# Hello!
# Hello!
# Hello!
```

Context Managers

Context managers are used to manage resources in a way that ensures proper acquisition and release of resources. The `with` statement in Python simplifies the management of resources like files, network connections, and locks.

1. Using `with` Statement:

The `with` statement ensures that resources are properly released after their use.

```
with open('example.txt', 'w') as file:
    file.write('Hello, World!')

# The file is automatically closed
when the block is exited
```

2. Creating Custom Context Managers:

You can create custom context managers using classes with `__enter__` and `__exit__` methods or using the `contextlib` module.

– **Using Classes:**

```
class MyContextManager:
    def __enter__(self):
        print("Entering the context")
        return self

    def __exit__(self, exc_type, exc_value, traceback):
```

```
        print("Exiting the context")

with MyContextManager() as manager:
    print("Inside the context")
# Outputs:
# Entering the context
# Inside the context
# Exiting the context
```

— **Using** `contextlib` **Module**:

```
from contextlib import contextmanager

@contextmanager
def my_context_manager():
    print("Entering the context")
    yield
    print("Exiting the context")

with my_context_manager():
    print("Inside the context")
# Outputs:
# Entering the context
# Inside the context
# Exiting the context
```

Metaclasses

Metaclasses are a powerful but advanced feature in Python. They are classes of classes, meaning that they define how classes behave. You can use metaclasses to modify or extend the behaviour of classes.

1. Basic Metaclass Example:

A metaclass is defined by inheriting from the `type` class.

```
class MyMeta(type):
    def __new__(cls, name, bases, dct):
        print(f"Creating class {name}")
        return super().__new__(cls, name, bases, dct)

class MyClass(metaclass=MyMeta):
    pass

# Outputs:
# Creating class MyClass
```

2. Customising Class Creation:

You can customise the creation and initialisation of classes using metaclasses.

```
class SingletonMeta(type):
    _instances = {}
    def __call__(cls, *args, **kwargs):
        if cls not in cls._instances:
```

```
        cls._instances[cls] =
super().__call__(*args, **kwargs)
        return cls._instances[cls]

class
Singleton(metaclass=SingletonMeta):
    pass

a = Singleton()
b = Singleton()

print(a is b)   # Outputs: True
```

Concurrency and Parallelism

Concurrency and parallelism are essential for improving the performance of programs by executing tasks simultaneously. Python provides several ways to achieve concurrency and parallelism, including threading, multiprocessing, and asynchronous programming.

1. Threading:

Threading allows you to run multiple threads (smaller units of process) concurrently within a single process.

```
import threading

def print_numbers():
    for i in range(5):
        print(i)

# Create two threads
```

```
thread1 = threading.Thread(target=print_numbers)
thread2 = threading.Thread(target=print_numbers)

# Start the threads
thread1.start()
thread2.start()

# Wait for the threads to finish
thread1.join()
thread2.join()
```

2. Multiprocessing:

Multiprocessing allows you to run multiple processes concurrently, each with its own memory space.

```
import multiprocessing

def print_numbers():
    for i in range(5):
        print(i)

# Create two processes
process1 = multiprocessing.Process(target=print_numbers)
```

```
process2 = 
multiprocessing.Process(target=print_
numbers)

# Start the processes
process1.start()
process2.start()

# Wait for the processes to finish
process1.join()
process2.join()
```

3. Asynchronous Programming:

Asynchronous programming allows you to run tasks asynchronously using `asyncio` in Python.

```
import asyncio

async def print_numbers():
    for i in range(5):
        print(i)


        await asyncio.sleep(1)

# Create an event loop
loop = asyncio.get_event_loop()

# Run the coroutine
```

```
loop.run_until_complete(print_numbers
())
```

4. Combining Concurrency Techniques:

You can combine threading, multiprocessing, and asynchronous programming to achieve more complex concurrency patterns.

– **Threading and Multiprocessing**:

```
import threading
import multiprocessing

def print_numbers():
    for i in range(5):
        print(i)

def run_threading():
    thread1 = threading.Thread(target=print_numbers)
    thread2 = threading.Thread(target=print_numbers)
    thread1.start()
    thread2.start()
    thread1.join()
    thread2.join()

# Create a process
```

```
process = 
multiprocessing.Process(target=run_th
reading)
process.start()
process.join()
```

– **Asynchronous Programming with Threading**:

```
import asyncio
import threading

async def print_numbers():
    for i in range(5):
        print(i)
        await asyncio.sleep(1)

def run_asyncio():
    loop = asyncio.new_event_loop()
    asyncio.set_event_loop(loop)

loop.run_until_complete(print_numbers
())

thread = 
threading.Thread(target=run_asyncio)
thread.start()
thread.join()
```

Working with Data Classes

Data classes provide a simple way to create classes that primarily store data. Introduced in Python 3.7, data classes automatically generate special methods like __init__, __repr__, and __eq__.

1. Basic Data Class Example:

```
from dataclasses import dataclass

@dataclass
class Point:
    x: int
    y: int

p1 = Point(1, 2)
p2 = Point(1, 2)

print(p1)           # Outputs:
Point(x=1, y=2)
print(p1 == p2)     # Outputs: True
```

2. Default Values and Type Hints:

You can specify default values and type hints in data classes.

```
from dataclasses import dataclass

@dataclass
class Person:
    name: str
    age: int = 30
```

```
p1 = Person(name="Alice")
p2 = Person(name="Bob", age=25)

print(p1)   # Outputs:
Person(name='Alice', age=30)
print(p2)   # Outputs:
Person(name='Bob', age=25)
```

3. Immutable Data Classes:

You can create immutable data classes using the `frozen` parameter.

```
from dataclasses import dataclass

@dataclass(frozen=True)
class Point:
    x: int
    y: int

p = Point(1, 2)
# p.x = 3   # This will raise an error: FrozenInstanceError
```

Working with Type Hints

Type hints improve code readability and facilitate static type checking. Introduced in Python 3.5, type hints allow you to specify the expected types of function arguments and return values.

1. Basic Type Hints:

```
def greet(name: str) -> str:
    return f"Hello, {name}!"

print(greet("Alice"))    # Outputs: Hello, Alice!
```

2. Optional and Union Types:

Use `Optional` and `Union` from the `typing` module to specify multiple possible types.

```
from typing import Optional, Union

def get_length(item: Optional[Union[str, list]]) -> int:
    if item is None:
        return 0
    return len(item)

print(get_length("Hello"))    # Outputs: 5
print(get_length([1, 2, 3]))  # Outputs: 3
print(get_length(None))       # Outputs: 0
```

3. Type Aliases:

Create type aliases to simplify complex type hints.

```
from typing import List, Tuple

Coordinates = List[Tuple[int, int]]
```

```python
def print_coordinates(coords:
Coordinates) -> None:
    for x, y in coords:
        print(f"({x}, {y})")

print_coordinates([(1, 2), (3, 4),
(5, 6)])
# Outputs:
# (1, 2)
# (3, 4)
# (5, 6)
```

4. Typed Dictionaries:

Use `TypedDict` to create dictionaries with specific types for keys and values.

```python
from typing import TypedDict

class Point(TypedDict):
    x: int
    y: int

point: Point = {'x': 1, 'y': 2}
print(point)   # Outputs: {'x': 1, 'y': 2}
```

Working with Generators

Generators provide an efficient way to create iterators. They allow you to yield values one at a time, suspending and resuming their state between each value.

1. Basic Generator Example:

```
def count_up_to(max: int):
    count = 1
    while count <= max:
        yield count
        count += 1

for number in count_up_to(5):
    print(number)
# Outputs:
# 1
# 2
# 3
# 4
# 5
```

2. Generator Expressions:

Generator expressions provide a concise way to create generators.

```
squares = (x * x for x in range(5))
for square in squares:
    print(square)
# Outputs:
# 0
# 1
# 4
# 9
# 16
```

3. Using `yield from`:

The `yield from` statement is used to delegate part of a generator's operations to another generator.

```
def subgenerator():
    yield 1
    yield 2

def main_generator():
    yield from subgenerator()
    yield 3

for value in main_generator():
    print(value)
# Outputs:
# 1
# 2
# 3
```

Practical Example: Building a Web Scraper

To solidify your understanding of these advanced topics, let's build a web scraper using OOP, decorators, context managers, and concurrency.

1. **Creating a Web Scraper Class:**

We'll create a web scraper class that fetches and parses web pages.

```
import requests
```

```python
from bs4 import BeautifulSoup

class WebScraper:
    def __init__(self, base_url):
        self.base_url = base_url

    def fetch_page(self, url):
        response = requests.get(url)
        return response.text

    def parse_page(self, html):
        soup = BeautifulSoup(html, 'html.parser')
        return soup

    def scrape(self, path):
        url = self.base_url + path
        html = self.fetch_page(url)
        return self.parse_page(html)
```

2. **Using Decorators for Logging:**

We'll add a decorator to log the scraping process.

```python
def log_scraping(func):
    def wrapper(*args, **kwargs):
        print(f"Scraping {args[1]}")
        result = func(*args, **kwargs)
        print("Scraping completed")
```

```
            return result
        return wrapper


class WebScraper:
    def __init__(self, base_url):
        self.base_url = base_url

    @log_scraping
    def scrape(self, path):
        url = self.base_url + path
        html = self.fetch_page(url)
        return self.parse_page(html)
```

3. Using Context Managers for Resource Management:

We'll use a context manager to handle the session.

```
from contextlib import contextmanager

@contextmanager
def session_scope():
    session = requests.Session()
    yield session
    session.close()

class WebScraper:
    def __init__(self, base_url):
        self.base_url = base_url
```

```
def fetch_page(self, url):
    with session_scope() as session:
        response = session.get(url)
        return response.text
```

4. Using Concurrency for Efficient Scraping:

We'll use threading to scrape multiple pages concurrently.

```
import threading

class WebScraper:
    def __init__(self, base_url):
        self.base_url = base_url

    def fetch_page(self, url):
        with session_scope() as session:
            response = session.get(url)
            return response.text

    def parse_page(self, html):
        soup = BeautifulSoup(html, 'html.parser')
        return soup

    @log_scraping
```

```python
    def scrape(self, path):
        url = self.base_url + path
        html = self.fetch_page(url)
        return self.parse_page(html)

    def scrape_multiple(self, paths):
        threads = []
        for path in paths:
            thread = 
threading.Thread(target=self.scrape, args=(path,))
            threads.append(thread)
            thread.start()

        for thread in threads:
            thread.join()

# Usage
scraper = WebScraper("https://example.com")
scraper.scrape_multiple(["/page1", "/page2", "/page3"])
```

Conclusion

In this chapter, we explored several advanced topics in Python, including object-oriented programming (OOP), decorators, context managers, metaclasses, concurrency, and parallelism. We also discussed working with data classes, type hints, and generators. By mastering these advanced concepts, you'll be able to write more efficient, scalable, and maintainable code. As you continue to practice and apply these techniques in real-world scenarios, you'll find that Python provides a robust and flexible environment for tackling complex programming challenges.

Chapter 12: Practical Projects and Applications

Introduction

Python is an incredibly versatile programming language that can be used to build a wide range of applications. In this chapter, we will explore several practical projects that showcase Python's capabilities. These projects will span various domains, including web development, data analysis, automation, and machine learning. By working through these examples, you'll gain hands-on experience and develop a deeper understanding of how to apply Python to real-world problems.

Project 1: Building a Simple Web Application with Flask

Flask is a lightweight web framework for Python that allows you to build web applications quickly and easily.

1. Setting Up Flask:

First, you need to install Flask. You can do this using pip:

```
pip install Flask
```

2. Creating a Basic Flask Application:

Let's create a simple web application that displays a welcome message.

```
from flask import Flask
```

```
app = Flask(__name__)

@app.route('/')
def home():
    return "Welcome to my web application!"

if __name__ == '__main__':
    app.run(debug=True)
```

Save this code in a file named app.py. Run the application using the command:

```
python app.py
```

Open your browser and navigate to http://127.0.0.1:5000/ to see the welcome message.

3. Creating Dynamic Web Pages:

Flask allows you to create dynamic web pages using templates. Let's create a template that displays a personalised greeting.

Create a folder named templates and a file named greeting.html inside it with the following content:

```html
<!DOCTYPE html>
<html>
<head>
    <title>Greeting</title>
</head>
<body>
    <h1>Hello, {{ name }}!</h1>
```

```
</body>
</html>
```

Modify app.py to render the template:

```
from flask import Flask, render_template

app = Flask(__name__)

@app.route('/')
def home():
    return "Welcome to my web application!"

@app.route('/greet/<name>')
def greet(name):
    return render_template('greeting.html', name=name)

if __name__ == '__main__':
    app.run(debug=True)
```

Navigate to http://127.0.0.1:5000/greet/YourName to see the personalised greeting.

Project 2: Data Analysis with Pandas

Pandas is a powerful data analysis library in Python. Let's use Pandas to analyse a dataset and gain insights from it.

1. **Loading the Data:**

We'll use a dataset of movies for this example. First, you need to install Pandas:

```
pip install pandas
```

Download a CSV file containing movie data and load it into a Pandas DataFrame:

```
import pandas as pd

# Load the dataset
df = pd.read_csv('movies.csv')

# Display the first few rows
print(df.head())
```

2. Cleaning the Data:

Data cleaning is an essential step in data analysis. Let's handle missing values and remove duplicates.

```
# Check for missing values
print(df.isnull().sum())

# Fill missing values
df['Revenue'] = df['Revenue'].fillna(df['Revenue'].mean())

# Remove duplicates
df = df.drop_duplicates()

# Display the cleaned dataset
```

```
print(df.head())
```

3. Analysing the Data:
Perform various analyses to gain insights from the data.

– Summary Statistics:

```
# Display summary statistics
print(df.describe())
```

– Top 10 Highest-Grossing Movies:

```
# Find the top 10 highest-grossing movies
top_grossing = df.nlargest(10, 'Revenue')
print(top_grossing[['Title', 'Revenue']])
```

– Average Rating by Genre:

```
# Calculate the average rating by genre
avg_rating_by_genre = df.groupby('Genre')['Rating'].mean()
print(avg_rating_by_genre)
```

Project 3: Automating Tasks with Python

Python can be used to automate repetitive tasks, saving time and effort. Let's create a script to automate sending emails.

1. Setting Up:

You'll need to install the `smtplib` library, which is included in the Python standard library, and `email` for constructing the email.

2. Writing the Script:

Here's a script to send an email using Gmail's SMTP server:

```
import smtplib
from email.mime.multipart import MIMEMultipart
from email.mime.text import MIMEText

def send_email(subject, body, to_email):
    from_email = "your_email@gmail.com"
    password = "your_password"

    # Create the email
    msg = MIMEMultipart()
    msg['From'] = from_email
    msg['To'] = to_email
    msg['Subject'] = subject

    # Attach the email body
    msg.attach(MIMEText(body, 'plain'))
```

```
    # Connect to the Gmail SMTP
server
    server =
smtplib.SMTP('smtp.gmail.com', 587)
    server.starttls()
    server.login(from_email,
password)

    # Send the email
    server.sendmail(from_email,
to_email, msg.as_string())

    # Disconnect from the server
    server.quit()

# Usage
send_email("Test Email", "This is a
test email.",
"recipient_email@gmail.com")
```

Replace your_email@gmail.com and your_password with your Gmail credentials, and recipient_email@gmail.com with the recipient's email address.

3. Scheduling the Script:

You can schedule the script to run at specific times using the schedule library.

```
pip install schedule
```

```
import schedule
import time

def job():
    send_email("Scheduled Email",
"This is a scheduled email.",
"recipient_email@gmail.com")

# Schedule the job every day at 9 AM
schedule.every().day.at("09:00").do(j
ob)

while True:
    schedule.run_pending()
    time.sleep(1)
```

Project 4: Building a Machine Learning Model

Machine learning involves training models on data to make predictions. Let's build a simple machine learning model using Scikit-learn.

1. Setting Up:
Install Scikit-learn using pip:

```
pip install scikit-learn
```

2. Preparing the Data:
We'll use the Iris dataset for this example.

```
from sklearn.datasets import load_iris
```

```
from sklearn.model_selection import
train_test_split

# Load the dataset
iris = load_iris()
X, y = iris.data, iris.target

# Split the data into training and
testing sets
X_train, X_test, y_train, y_test =
train_test_split(X, y, test_size=0.3,
random_state=42)
```

3. Training the Model:
We'll use a Random Forest classifier for this example.

```
from sklearn.ensemble import
RandomForestClassifier

# Create and train the model
model =
RandomForestClassifier(n_estimators=100)
model.fit(X_train, y_train)
```

4. Evaluating the Model:
Evaluate the model's performance using accuracy and a classification report.

```
from sklearn.metrics import
accuracy_score, classification_report
```

```
# Make predictions
y_pred = model.predict(X_test)

# Calculate accuracy
accuracy = accuracy_score(y_test,
y_pred)
print(f"Accuracy: {accuracy}")

# Print classification report
print(classification_report(y_test,
y_pred,
target_names=iris.target_names))
```

5. Saving and Loading the Model:

Save the trained model to a file and load it later for making predictions.

```
import joblib

# Save the model
joblib.dump(model,
'random_forest_model.pkl')

# Load the model
loaded_model =
joblib.load('random_forest_model.pkl'
)

# Make predictions with the loaded
model
```

```
y_pred_loaded =
loaded_model.predict(X_test)
print(f"Accuracy of loaded model:
{accuracy_score(y_test,
y_pred_loaded)}")
```

Project 5: Creating a RESTful API with Flask and Flask-RESTful

APIs allow different software systems to communicate with each other. Let's create a RESTful API using Flask and Flask-RESTful.

1. Setting Up:
Install Flask and Flask-RESTful using pip:

```
pip install Flask Flask-RESTful
```

2. Creating the API:
Here's an example of a simple API that manages a list of books.

```
from flask import Flask, request
from flask_restful import Resource, Api

app = Flask(__name__)
api = Api(app)

books = []

class Book(Resource):
    def get(self):
```

```
        return books

    def post(self):
        new_book = request.json
        books.append(new_book)
        return new_book, 201

api.add_resource(Book, '/books')

if __name__ == '__main__':
    app.run(debug=True)
```

3. Testing the API:

You can test the API using tools like Postman or `curl`.

– **Get all books:**

```
curl http://127.0.0.1:5000/books
```

– **Add a new book:**

```
curl -X POST -H "Content-Type: application/json" -d '{"title": "The Great Gatsby", "author": "F. Scott Fitzgerald"}' http://127.0.0.1:5000/books
```

Conclusion

In this chapter, we explored several practical projects and applications using Python, including building a simple web application with Flask, performing data analysis with Pandas, automating tasks with Python, building a machine learning model with Scikit-learn, and creating a RESTful API with Flask and Flask-RESTful. These projects demonstrate the versatility and power of Python in various domains. By working through these examples, you gain hands-on experience and develop a deeper understanding of how to apply Python to solve real-world problems. As you continue to practice and build more projects, you'll become more proficient in Python and be able to tackle more complex challenges.

Chapter 13: Best Practices and Further Resources

Introduction

As you advance in your Python programming journey, adhering to best practices becomes essential for writing clean, efficient, and maintainable code. This chapter covers various best practices, including coding standards, code organisation, testing, debugging, and performance optimisation. Additionally, it provides resources for further learning to help you continue improving your Python skills.

Coding Standards and Style Guidelines

Following coding standards and style guidelines ensures consistency and readability across your codebase. The Python community has established a set of conventions known as PEP 8.

1. PEP 8:

PEP 8 is the official style guide for Python code. It covers various aspects of writing Python code, including naming conventions, code layout, and documentation.

- **Indentation:**

Use 4 spaces per indentation level.

```
def my_function():
    if True:
```

```
print("Hello, World!")
```

- **Line Length:**

Limit lines to 79 characters.

```
def my_function():
    # This is a very long comment that exceeds the maximum line length of 79 characters, so it should be wrapped.
    pass
```

- **Blank Lines:**

Use blank lines to separate top-level function and class definitions.

```
class MyClass:
    def method_one(self):
        pass

    def method_two(self):
        pass
```

- **Imports:**

Import statements should be placed at the top of the file, grouped, and ordered.

```
import os
import sys

from collections import defaultdict
```

2. Naming Conventions:

Consistent naming conventions make your code more readable and understandable.

– Variables and Functions:

Use lowercase words separated by underscores.

```
my_variable = 10

def my_function():
    pass
```

– Classes:

Use CapitalizedWords (PascalCase).

```
class MyClass:
    pass
```

– Constants:

Use uppercase words separated by underscores.

```
MY_CONSTANT = 42
```

3. Docstrings:

Use docstrings to document your functions, classes, and modules. Follow the PEP 257 conventions for docstrings.

```
def my_function(param1, param2):
    """
    Brief description of what the function does.

    Args:
        param1 (int): Description of param1.
        param2 (str): Description of param2.

    Returns:
        bool: Description of the return value.
    """
    return True
```

Code Organisation and Modularisation

Organising your code into modules and packages improves maintainability and reusability.

1. Modules and Packages:

A module is a single Python file, and a package is a collection of modules in a directory with an __init__.py file.

220

- **Creating a Module:**

Save the following code in a file named `my_module.py`.

```python
def my_function():
    print("Hello from my_module!")
```

- **Creating a Package:**

Create a directory structure as follows:

```
my_package/
    __init__.py
    module_one.py
    module_two.py
```

In `module_one.py`:

```python
def function_one():
    print("Function one from module_one")
```

In `module_two.py`:

```python
def function_two():
    print("Function two from module_two")
```

In `__init__.py`:

```python
from .module_one import function_one
```

```
from .module_two import function_two
```

- **Using the Package:**

```
from my_package import function_one, function_two

function_one()
function_two()
```

2. Structuring a Python Project:

A well-structured project directory improves readability and maintainability.

```
my_project/
    my_package/
        __init__.py
        module_one.py
        module_two.py
    tests/
        test_module_one.py
        test_module_two.py
    docs/
        index.md
    README.md
    setup.py
    requirements.txt
```

Testing and Debugging

Testing ensures that your code works as expected, and debugging helps identify and fix issues.

1. Unit Testing:

Unit testing involves testing individual components of your code. The `unittest` module is the built-in library for unit testing in Python.

- **Creating Unit Tests:**

```
import unittest
from my_package.module_one import function_one

class TestModuleOne(unittest.TestCase):
    def test_function_one(self):

self.assertEqual(function_one(),
"Function one from module_one")

if __name__ == '__main__':
    unittest.main()
```

2. Test Coverage:

Test coverage measures how much of your code is tested. The `coverage` package helps track test coverage.

```
pip install coverage
coverage run -m unittest discover
```

```
coverage report
```

3. Debugging:
The `pdb` module is the built-in debugger for Python.

- **Using** pdb:

```
import pdb

def buggy_function():
    pdb.set_trace()
    x = 10
    y = 0
    result = x / y
    return result

buggy_function()
```

4. Logging:
Logging helps track events in your code and is useful for debugging and monitoring.

- **Using the** `logging` **Module:**

```
import logging

logging.basicConfig(level=logging.INFO)

def my_function():
```

```
    logging.info("This is an
informational message")
    logging.warning("This is a
warning message")
    logging.error("This is an error
message")

my_function()
```

Performance Optimisation

Optimising the performance of your code can make it run faster and more efficiently.

1. Profiling:

Profiling helps identify performance bottlenecks in your code. The `cProfile` module is a built-in profiler for Python.

- **Using** `cProfile`:

```
import cProfile

def my_function():
    result = 0
    for i in range(1000000):
        result += i
    return result

cProfile.run('my_function()')
```

2. Optimising Code:

Use efficient data structures and algorithms to improve performance.

- **Using List Comprehensions:**

```
# Inefficient
squares = []
for i in range(10):
    squares.append(i * i)

# Efficient
squares = [i * i for i in range(10)]
```

- **Using Built-in Functions:**

```
# Inefficient
total = 0
for i in range(1000):
    total += i

# Efficient
total = sum(range(1000))
```

- **Avoiding Unnecessary Calculations:**

```
import math
```

```
def compute():
    for i in range(1000):
        result = math.sqrt(100)

# Store the result of the computation
outside the loop
def compute_optimized():
    result = math.sqrt(100)
    for i in range(1000):
        pass
```

3. Using C Extensions:

For performance-critical code, consider using C extensions or libraries like `Cython` to compile Python code to C.

- **Using Cython:**

```
pip install cython
```

Create a file named `my_module.pyx`:

```
def compute(int n):
    cdef int i
    cdef double result = 0
    for i in range(n):
        result += i
    return result
```

Compile the module:

```
cythonize -i my_module.pyx
```

Use the compiled module:

```
import my_module
print(my_module.compute(1000))
```

Best Practices for Collaborative Development

Working effectively in a team requires good practices for collaboration, version control, and documentation.

1. Version Control:

Version control systems like Git help manage changes to your codebase and collaborate with others.

– **Using Git:**

```
git init
git add .
git commit -m "Initial commit"
git remote add origin https://github.com/yourusername/yourrepository.git
git push -u origin master
```

2. Code Reviews:

Conduct regular code reviews to ensure code quality and share knowledge among team members.

3. Continuous Integration:

Set up continuous integration (CI) to automatically run tests and checks on your codebase. Tools like Travis CI and GitHub Actions can help.

– **Setting Up GitHub Actions:**

Create a `.github/workflows/python-app.yml` file:

```
name: Python application

on: [push]

jobs:
  build:

    runs-on: ubuntu-latest

    steps:
    - uses: actions/checkout@v2
    - name: Set up Python
      uses: actions/setup-python@v2
      with:
        python-version: 3.x
    - name: Install dependencies
      run: |
        python -m pip install --upgrade pip

        pip install -r requirements.txt
    - name: Run tests
```

```
run: |
  pytest
```

4. Documentation:

Good documentation is crucial for maintaining and sharing your code.

- **Using Docstrings:**

```
def my_function(param1, param2):
    """
    Brief description of what the function does.

    Args:
        param1 (int): Description of param1.
        param2 (str): Description of param2.

    Returns:
        bool: Description of the return value.
    """
    return True
```

- **Using Sphinx:**

Sphinx is a tool for generating documentation from your code.

```
pip install sphinx
sphinx-quickstart
```

Edit the `conf.py` file to include your project modules:

```
import os
import sys
sys.path.insert(0,
os.path.abspath('../src'))
```

Create reStructuredText (`.rst`) files for your modules and build the documentation:

```
sphinx-apidoc -o docs/source/ ../src
sphinx-build -b html docs/source/ docs/build/
```

View the generated documentation in the `docs/build/` directory.

Further Resources

Continuing to learn and explore is crucial for advancing your Python skills. Here are some valuable resources for further learning:

1. **Online Courses:**

   – **Coursera:**

   – **edX:**

   – **Udemy:**

2. Official Documentation:

– **Python Documentation:**

The official Python documentation is an excellent resource for learning about the language and its standard library.
Python Documentation
https://docs.python.org/3/

3. Community and Forums:

– **Stack Overflow:**

A popular Q&A site for programming questions.
Stack Overflow
https://stackoverflow.com/

– **Reddit:**

The Python subreddit is a place to discuss Python-related topics.
Reddit Python
https://www.reddit.com/r/Python/

– **Python Discord:**

4. Open Source Contributions:

Contributing to open-source projects is a great way to improve your skills and give back to the community. You can find projects to contribute to on GitHub.

– **GitHub:**

Explore repositories and contribute to open-source projects.
GitHub
https://github.com/

Conclusion

In this chapter, we covered best practices for writing clean, efficient, and maintainable Python code. We explored coding standards, code organisation, testing, debugging, performance optimisation, and collaborative development practices. Additionally, we provided resources for further learning to help you continue improving your Python skills. By adhering to these best practices and continually learning, you'll become a more proficient and effective Python programmer, capable of tackling complex projects and contributing to the broader programming community.

Printed in Great Britain
by Amazon